Ruby Slippers

FAIRY TALES MY MOTHER TOLD ME, SECRETS I NEVER SHARED

2ND EDITION

MICHELLE DAVIS-NEWELL

SCRIBERITE
PUBLISHING LLC

Acknowledgments

Revamping this second edition has been a true labor of love, and bringing it to life has been nothing short of extraordinary. So much has changed in my life since the initial release, and it felt only right to update and complete this work to reflect those transformative experiences.

I would like to express my deepest gratitude to the following individuals for their unwavering love, support, and commitment, not only to this project but to so many other endeavors along the way:

To my children—Michelle, Renee, Pierre, and Joshua—you are and will always be my greatest source of strength. Being your parent has been the most challenging and rewarding on-the-job learning experience of my life. I know I've made mistakes along the way, yet you love me unconditionally. Thank you for teaching me as much as I've tried to teach you.

To my beautiful bonus children, Lauren, Jamilah, Justin, Jordan, and Erin—you are the sweetest angels a bonus mom could ever pray for. I love you all dearly and cherish the bonds we've built.

To my grandchildren, who inspire me more with each passing day. From our first grandchild to our newest little angel, I am blessed to have you all in my life. Maliq, the Pegasus; Malia, Zaria, Zoe, Nyla, Mesziah, Landon, Nicalli, Aya (Papaya), and Aspen—you fill my heart with joy and remind me every day why it's important to keep pushing forward.

To my best friend, Michelle Chambers—thank you for being my "Ace " since we were ten years old. You've always stood by me, through the highs and lows, and have been my "psychologist" during my times of need. Your friendship means the world to me.

To the original "team" who helped make the first edition of this book a reality—my editors Marilyn Weishaar (The Weis Revise) and Carla M. Dean (U Can Mark My Word)—your professional expertise and heartfelt encouragement shaped the original project into something beautiful. I am eternally grateful for the care and dedication you brought to the first iteration of this work.

To all my family members and close friends who constantly offered words of encouragement along the way—thank you. Your love and support have been the wind beneath my wings.

And finally, saving the best for last: my husband, Keith Newell. You have been my rock, my confidant, and my greatest champion. Thank you for everything—from your creative insights to your unshakable support. Without you, this project would have been immeasurably harder to complete. You make everything feel possible.

If I have overlooked anyone, please blame it on my mind (and the constraints of this space!), not my heart. Every single bit of support counts, and none of it goes unnoticed.

Dedication

When I think about strong women, there are many who come to mind. However, there is one woman who epitomizes true strength in every sense of the word. That woman is my mother, the late Izora Davis.

Most probably view their mother as the strongest woman they know, especially if she raised them in turbulent situations and environments. I watched my mother struggle with being a young single parent as I grew up, and I saw her blossom into a strong, courageous soul who fought tirelessly in advocating for others.

This is hard to admit, but for years, I resented her because I wanted to blame her for my failures. While a teen, I had the expectation that it was her responsibility to make me into the success she told me I could become. Isn't that always the way with teenagers? That feeling of unfettered entitlement that parents owe them the world and everything in it. I learned the hard way that parents don't turn their children into successes; they simply provide the nourishment the ego needs to get there.

I didn't get it back then. As a teenage parent, my mother went through all kinds of hell and pain - literally and figuratively, which impacted her life, as well as mine and my brother's. Some of those same struggles cycled down to me when I entered adulthood.

Because of the impact she made on my life, I dedicate this book to her, telling her spirit what I wish I could have shared with her when she was alive. There are some who may read this and take offense with a lot of the truths disclosed here because of the relationship they had with her. It is because of those few that I was hesitant to discuss some of these details.

However, my mother's spirit encouraged me, reminding me that she was not without flaws. It wasn't her mistakes that made her great; it was her growth. This is the biggest and greatest gift she passed down to me – she taught me how to grow past my failures.

I screwed up a lot in my life, making decisions that not only impacted me, but affected my children. However, I grew stronger from those errors, and I did so by acknowledging my mistakes and making every effort to learn from them. She taught me all of this - not with words, but by her actions. When the reality of everything she ever taught me finally sunk in, it was too late to talk to her about it, and to thank her. She passed away suddenly in 2006.

There are a lot who are grateful to my mother, and the community she fought for came together and returned the favor.

In the summer of 2012, a park was co-named after her and another community activist for their contributions of ensuring the rights of others were protected. Izora took on the public housing authority of Chicago, politicians, and bureaucrats alike to guarantee that the rights of public housing residents were acknowledged and respected. She always believed it didn't matter where one lived or what his or her socio-economic situation was; everyone had a right to fair and equal treatment.

This is how she lived her life – fighting for others, even if it meant putting herself in harm's way. She is a glowing example that despite our failures, we can make a difference in this world.

I also dedicate this book to women and girls everywhere. It is my hope that someone reading this will gain the courage to talk to their mother, father, or someone close to them about issues they faced or may be going through. I pray that any child who is being molested, bullied, or teased finds the courage to speak up. I pray that any woman or man who has been abused learns to rid themselves of misplaced guilt, shame, or resentment so they can begin to heal.

I encourage everyone to never wait until it's too late to seek help.

Trigger Warnings

This memoir addresses sensitive and potentially triggering topics, including but not limited to:

- **Childhood Trauma and Abuse:** Discussions of molestation, neglect, and bullying that may evoke emotional responses.
- **Domestic Violence:** Accounts of physical, emotional, and psychological abuse within relationships.
- **Substance Abuse and Addiction:** Depictions of drug addiction and its impact on individuals and families.
- **Mental Health Challenges:** Reflections on depression, grief, and coping with the loss of loved ones.
- **Loss and Grief:** The emotional impact of losing close family members and navigating life afterward.

These subjects are presented with honesty and care as part of my personal journey, but they may be challenging for some readers. If you are sensitive to these topics, please proceed with caution and take breaks as needed.

Remember, it's okay to step away and seek support if you find yourself feeling overwhelmed. If you or someone you know is struggling with related issues, consider reaching out to a trusted individual or professional resource.

Thank you for choosing to read Ruby Slippers: Fairy Tales My Mother Told Me, Secrets I Never Shared. My hope is that this memoir will inspire healing, resilience, and strength for those walking their own unique paths.

– Michelle Davis-Newell

Prologue

The first time I saw The Wiz as a little girl in 1978, I was completely mesmerized. It wasn't just a movie; it was an experience. Watching Dorothy journey through a world that was unfamiliar, unpredictable, and dangerous felt like a mirror to my own life. But what made it magical wasn't just the story—it was the music.

Every beat, every lyric, every melody resonated in my soul. Music was already my sanctuary, but The Wiz showed me how it could tell stories, heal wounds, and connect us to something greater than ourselves. And for the first time, I saw characters who looked like me navigating struggles with resilience and strength. It felt like watching a reflection of my own dreams and fears.

Then there were the ruby slippers. Those sparkling shoes weren't just Dorothy's ticket home; they were a symbol of power, self-discovery, and courage. As I sat wide-eyed watching with my mother, I didn't fully understand it at the time, but I was drawn to the way Dorothy found her strength along the yellow brick road. Her journey was messy and filled with obstacles, but she kept going. Those slippers were a reminder that, even when we feel lost, we carry the power to find our way within us.

Cue 'Ease on down the road.'

That's what this book is about: finding your way home. Not the physical place, but the emotional and spiritual home inside yourself. Like Dorothy, I've wandered through some dark, scary places. I've encountered my share of witches, flying monkeys, and shady wizards, all promising something they couldn't deliver. But through it all, I discovered what Dorothy learned at the end of her journey: the power to heal, to thrive, to break free from cycles, was with me all along. I just needed to believe it.

Life has a way of throwing its version of Oz at you. You think you're walking a straight path, and suddenly you're in the middle of a storm, swept away from everything familiar. You land somewhere new, where nothing feels safe, and the road ahead seems impossible to navigate. For me, those storms came in the form of heartbreak, trauma, and loss—each one pulling me further away from the life I always dreamed of achieving.

While traveling down life's yellow brick road, I encountered obstacles that threatened to destroy me. But many of those experiences I never shared with a soul. Keeping painful secrets from those you love, no matter the reason, doesn't protect them—it hurts them. And it hurts you even more.

Those secrets stifle your growth in ways you don't realize until years later, when you're still carrying them like bricks in a bag you forgot to put down. I know because I've lived it. I spent years holding onto the kind of pain that makes you feel like you're walking barefoot on that road, with every step cutting deep.

As I sit here revisiting this book, I can't help but ask myself, "Is this update even necessary? Is it worth it?" The original was published in 2013, seven years after my mother passed. Since then, life has spun me around like a twister, dropping me in places I never imagined I'd be.

I've endured joys, such as returning to school and earning my bachelor's degree; and heartaches, including the devastating loss of my brother—a pain that still sneaks up on me, catching me off guard with tears at the most unexpected moments.

But does all of that warrant a new edition of the same book? I mean, life keeps life'ing for all of us, right?

The truth is, this update isn't about catching up on my life's latest events. If it were, I'd be updating this book every year! Instead, it's about revisiting the journey, reflecting on what I've learned, and offering a little more wisdom to the women walking their own yellow brick roads.

My husband and I recently started our own publishing company, and releasing this book under our imprint feels like the perfect way to re-ignite the message I originally set out to share.

I wrote this book with a singular purpose: to light a fire under you. Yes, you, the person reading these words right now. My goal has always been to inspire women to let go of the emotional and psychological baggage that weighs us down— the kind that keeps you up at night, gripping your throat like it's got you in a chokehold. I want you to realize that you've had the ruby slippers on all along.

Let's be honest—most of the junk we carry comes from letting our emotions lead the way. Love and compassion? We've got those in spades. For our kids, and especially for our mate. But letting emotions drive every decision we make? That's a recipe for disaster.

How many times have you or someone you know cried, "But I love him!" as if love alone justifies staying in chaos? I've been there too—crying into my pillow after ignoring every red flag, only to look back later and wonder, "How did I not see that mess coming?"

But love and the decisions we make while in the throes of chaos aren't the only thing that weighs us down. We cling to grudges, secrets, and past hurts like they're some kind of emotional safety net. I carried so much baggage, it felt like I was dragging a sack of cement everywhere I went. It was heavy, unrelenting, and damn near impossible to move.

It took me years to understand that holding onto all that emotional weight wasn't helping me. It was holding me back, blocking my blessings. You'd be surprised how heavy guilt, shame, and secrecy can feel when you carry them for too long.

I kept so much hidden from the people who could've helped me—my mom, my friends. Hell, probably Oprah if I'd reached out in time. But those wasted opportunities delayed the growth I so desperately needed. Who knows where I'd be today if I'd let go sooner?

Instead of confronting my issues, I tried to outrun them. I thought if I buried my painful history deep enough or put enough distance between me and the memories, they'd simply disappear. But here's the truth: the past doesn't just vanish. It's like the Wicked Witch of the West—always lurking in the shadows, waiting for the perfect moment to leap out and remind you she's still there, demanding to be dealt with.

As you'll see in this book, I've got stories. But don't we all? The more I talk to other women, the more I realize my struggles aren't unique. We all have baggage, and we need to stop ignoring it. More importantly, we need to stop judging each other for it.

Being a woman is hard enough in a world built to make things harder for us. And when we add in our own divisions—race, hair texture, body size, beauty standards—it's no wonder we feel so isolated and alone.

Now more than ever, we need to lift each other up and build a sisterhood. There's already enough negativity in the world. Sure, men have their struggles too, but let's be real—women catch it from every direction. Broken hearts? Check. Mistreated and misunderstood? Double check.

Society loves to pile on the pressure, and when we react, we're the ones labeled with the problem:

- "She's got an attitude."
- "She's bitter."
- "She's got issues."

Yes, sometimes we do have attitudes—who wouldn't, with all we deal with? But here's the truth: men have baggage too, yet no one's calling them names for it. The next time someone throws a judgment your way, remember this: no one knows what you've been through. No one knows your story.

- Maybe you've been the mom and the dad to your kids.
- Maybe you've held everything together while your world crumbled around you.
- Maybe you've been cheated on, disrespected, or taken for granted more times than you can count.

- Maybe you carry emotional, psychological, or physical scars no one can see—and you've had no one to help you heal.
- Maybe you're just plain tired of trying to make something out of nothing.

If you've been through all of that and are still standing, know there is nothing you can't overcome. Like Dorothy realized right before she clicked those beautiful, glittery ruby reds three times, you've got more strength than you realize. Once you tap into it, everything changes. No matter where you are in life, it's never too late to discover your power.

Life isn't a fairy tale or even a soulful musical—it's real, it's messy, and no one is coming to rescue us. We're not waiting on Prince Charming, and the Good Witch won't just show up to wave her wand. That's why we have to equip ourselves with wisdom, especially in relationships. The choices we make today can save us a world of pain tomorrow. And when the options seem limited, trust your intuition. It's there for a reason and won't steer you wrong.

This is especially true if you have children. Our kids watch us like we're the stars of their favorite show or the latest TikTok dance trend. That's why we need to be mindful of the "episodes" we let them see—especially our daughters. If we don't break cycles like abuse and trauma, they'll inherit them. Breaking the cycle starts with recognizing it for what it is—a chance to rewrite the story.

Ladies, we are resilient. Like Dorothy, we're the ones who face the witches, the flying monkeys, and the false wizards. And like her, we'll discover we've had the magic of the ruby slippers all along. The slippers didn't just sparkle—they symbolized her ability to get back home, her power to find her way even when the path seemed impossible. She just needed an awakening to realize it.

Today's woman is a force to be reckoned with. We've been muted long enough. Now we're awake, and we're ready to be heard.

The yellow brick road may be bumpy, winding, and filled with challenges, but we're walking it boldly. So watch out, world—the giants are awake, and we're stepping forward with purpose, one dazzling ruby-slippered step at a time.

One

Who defines a woman's worth? Is it society? Your family? The people you date? Men? Other women? Or is it your own experiences?

Sometimes, it's our experiences—shaping who we are or, better yet, who we will become. Let me tell you this: being a woman isn't just a box you check under "gender." It's a mindset, and it goes way beyond curves and lipstick. There's power in being a woman—a power we often don't even know we possess. I sure didn't. It wasn't until I was well into my thirties that I started recognizing my strength and finally felt comfortable in my own skin.

As a teen, I was awkward as hell. I didn't know how to "be" around anyone who wasn't related to me. I was that quiet girl who loved to read, could spell like a champ, and had a future so bright I was practically squinting. The adults around me could see the potential oozing out of me.

They just knew I was going to do great things, climb out of the ghetto, and make something of myself. The potential they saw was real—I was smart, talented, and capable. But life has a way of throwing monkey wrenches at all your plans until that shiny, hopeful future feels more like a broken-down car rusting in the driveway.

In my late teens and early twenties, people still saw that potential. They believed I could navigate life's bumpy roads with ease and live up to all the expectations that seemed to emanate off me. "You gon' be somebody!" they proclaimed, over and over again. And I wanted to be that person.

But here's the thing: nobody saw how lost I was. I spent years trying to balance who I was with who I was supposed to be, all while juggling everyone else's hopes and dreams for me. And you know what happens when you try to be everything for everyone? You get exhausted. Real quick. And then the balls start dropping.

Now, mix that exhaustion with trying to find your footing in a world that might have a few strikes against you—whether it's your gender, your race, or your relationship status (hello, single mothers!)—and it's like trying to walk up a hill covered in oil. Slippery, messy, and frustrating. Not to mention, falling on your ass hurts like hell, too.

When you're young, people love to tell you who you should be. They'll offer their visions of your future with the best of intentions. And when you stumble, it shatters something inside you. Their disappointment clings to you like a bad song stuck on repeat, and you wonder if you'll ever get it right.

If you're lucky, someone will say, "It's okay. You're gonna go through this. Just stay focused, don't give up, and you'll make it out on the other side." But what if no one says that? What if there's no guiding hand when life gets rocky? What if your emotional stability needs a push, but all you've got is silence or judgment?

Relying on others for emotional bailouts can be a tricky habit. Encouragement is great, don't get me wrong. But when it's depended on to function, you're setting yourself up for a tough time when it's not there. It's a hard truth, but life isn't always going to hand us the pep talk we're looking for.

Picking yourself up after a fall isn't easy—especially when you land waist-deep in disillusionment, heartache, and disappointment. I know because I've been there. The fairy tale love I thought was mine? A myth. The heartache from failed goals? Oh, it was my constant companion. And the disappointment in myself? That was daily. But then, I had a revelation: my life was mine to shape.

Let me say that again for the people in the back: my life was mine to shape. The moment I realized that, I found the confidence I needed to climb out of the rut I buried myself in. I learned to be my own cheerleader—the most important one I'd ever need.

Here's the thing: real growth starts when you take ownership of your failures. It's easy to blame circumstances or other people for the pain and setbacks, but the hard truth is, some of those stumbles are the result of our own choices. It took me a long time to face that. I had to dig deep, acknowledge some ugly realities, and confront the decisions I made when I was young and dumb.

When you're young, thinking before you act is about as easy as folding a fitted sheet. We've all heard adults preach about how we should be wise and think ahead, but when you're in the moment? That's the last thing on your mind. Impulse rules.

And maturity? For some, that only comes with time and a whole lot of "lessons learned" later in life.

As we grow older, we look back and opine, "If I knew then what I know now..." But let's face it, hindsight is a luxury. The environment you grow up in shapes you, sometimes limits you, and it takes willpower to break free from those limitations.

Sometimes I ask myself: If I could go back and change some of my poor decisions, would I? It's tempting to say yes, but honestly? I wouldn't. The choices I made, the mistakes I lived through, they shaped me into who I am today. They gave me wisdom. They taught me how to navigate the twists and turns life throws at you, and how to do better next time.

But—and this is a big but—there are a few moments, the deep and hurtful ones, that I wouldn't mind erasing. And there are some repeat episodes I'd never want to see again. But if those moments taught me something, I'd be hesitant to change them.

You see, I don't believe in wasting mistakes. My daughter Renee once said, "Having regrets means you didn't learn from the situation." And she's right. Regret stunts your growth. It holds you back. Growth comes from learning, even when that learning is painful.

When we cling to regrets, we allow self-loathing and bitterness to settle rent-free in our heart. Nothing good ever comes from that toxic cocktail. It's like shaking up a bottle of soda— pressure builds, emotions bubble over, and when it finally explodes, it's messy and impossible to contain. The fallout isn't just ugly—it's destructive.

Reflecting on the toughest times in my life, I try to pinpoint the emotions that drove my decisions. Confusion, sadness, feeling overwhelmed, depression—you name it. But you know what was missing? A healthy dose of anger. People say don't get angry, but I disagree. The right anger can fuel your determination. It can spark a fire inside you to move out of the dark place and never look back.

Here's the thing: there's a difference between anger and bitterness. Anger can motivate you. Bitterness? It just keeps you stuck. The point is to find the thing that makes you say, "This will never happen to me again." Then you make the changes to ensure it doesn't. Sometimes that means cutting out toxic elements in your life—and that includes people.

I was knocked down so many times by situations—some of my own making, others out of my control—that I almost stayed down. It's tempting to stay down, right? There's comfort in it. No risk of falling if you're already on the ground. But there's no growth in that.

No matter how many times you hit rock bottom, you've got to rise again—not just to survive, but to succeed. Success feels even more rewarding when it comes after you've fought your way back from the depths.

So, plant your hands firmly on the ground, summon every ounce of resolve, and push yourself up. Stand tall—not because the world demands perfection, but because it needs your authenticity, your resilience, and your voice. The world isn't waiting for you to be flawless—it's waiting for you to claim your strength and step boldly into it. You are needed, more than you know, and your light has the power to impact more lives than you could ever imagine.

Two

L osing a mother is a pain that does not go away easily. I often think about our last in-person conversation, just a few months before she passed in 2006. I had finally opened up to her about the struggles I was having with my live-in boyfriend at the time, who turned out to be a habitual cheater. He'd had us both fooled.

I didn't usually talk to her about things like that. Maybe it was because I didn't believe in running to her every time a relationship fell apart, or maybe I just wanted to handle it on my own.

By then, though, my mother had lived through her own share of heartache and growth, and she'd seen me mature into someone who was handling life better than I had before. She listened with patience and care, asking all the right questions. What I remember most is that she didn't try to give me advice, which was the right thing. I wasn't asking for her to solve my problems. I just wanted to talk to my mom, to share what I was going through, and to feel her presence.

That was the relationship we had grown into—a bond rooted in mutual understanding and respect. It brought us closer than ever, and I'm forever grateful we had the chance to reach that place. Still, there's so much more I wish I could tell her. So much I'd love to share—especially now.

If I could write her a letter in heaven, here's what I'd say.

> Dear Mama,
> You were right. Not because you told me so—you never had to. You weren't the mother to sit me down and give me advice in long lectures, or tell me how life would unfold. You were more of a "you'll learn" kind of teacher, the kind who believed some lessons are best experienced, not explained.
> And I get it now. I see what you were trying to show me, even though I had to learn it on my own, through painful struggles and experiences. Unfortunately, those lessons didn't come soon enough to prevent me from repeating some of the same cycles you went through. And, as I watched my own daughters grow, I fought hard to keep them from traveling down those same paths.
> You tried to show me; I tried to show and tell them. But I'm learning that life's lessons don't always come from show and tell. Sometimes, you just have to live through them. I see now that's what you were trying to show me all along.
> Witnessing the physical abuse you endured made sure I would never be with a man who

thought it was okay to lay a hand on me. But that didn't mean I escaped all the other forms of abuse—emotional, psychological—that left scars just as deep.

I've often wondered if these cycles are somehow genetic, passed down like a curse. Sometimes, it feels like no matter how hard we try to protect or prepare our children, certain patterns are destined to repeat themselves.

Your mother had her first child in her early teens, married young, and endured physical abuse from her husband. In the early to mid-1900s, that wasn't so unusual—but I'm sure it didn't make it any less painful for her.

Over time, life evolved, and the world changed, but the cycles didn't stop. Like so many women in our family, you repeated those same patterns. And they continued to pass down, generation after generation.

The thought of my grandchildren—your great-grandchildren and our future generations facing the same trials terrifies me. But I refuse to believe the apple has to fall close to the tree. With the right knowledge and guidance taught early, I know they can make better decisions and finally break these cycles.

We must talk about the hard stuff—the abuse, the hidden issues that silently shaped our lives. Ignoring these problems doesn't make them disappear. They don't vanish just because we don't speak them aloud. Instead, they fester, growing into new forms of pain, sometimes even more devastating than what came before.

It's also about passing down the strength to stand tall when life shakes your foundation. I look at the resilience you had, and the strength of the women who came before us, and I take comfort in knowing that no matter what comes our way, we come from a line of survivors. We can overcome anything.

I've learned that to truly resolve an issue, you have to get to the root of it. Focusing on the surface doesn't fix the core problem; it only masks it temporarily. Even when you think you've dealt with it, the residue of the actual issue will resurface in other ways. Problems, like weeds, need to be pulled up by the roots.

For me, that meant going back to the beginning—my childhood. As I look back on some of the darkest times in my life, I need to make one thing clear: I. Do not. Blame you. Not for any of it. You were a single teenage mother doing the best you could with what little you had. The 60s and 70s were harsh times, especially for people of color, and doubly so for those trapped in poverty.

Knowing that, I salute you for everything you did. For bringing me into this world, even when your own father threatened to kick you out of the house *if you did. You walked into the world defiantly, braving life's storms, learning each lesson the hard way.*

Damn. You were rock solid. I didn't realize it back then, but I see it now. I understand it.

I understand you.

Three

Mama's not the only one I wish I could talk to. We've all had those moments where we wish we could go back in time and give our younger selves a pep talk—maybe a hug, or just a little reassurance that everything will be okay. If I could do that, I'd send a letter to my thirteen-year-old self. It would go something like this:

> Dear Me,
> Hey Beautiful. Believe it or not, you're going to be okay. I know it doesn't feel like it right now. You've had a rough time growing up. When you were just nine years old, you lived through one of the scariest moments of your life—when your cousin found you out of it, barely conscious, after swallowing a handful of Mama's pills. You really tried it, didn't you? What brought you to that point?
> Was it the time you woke up in a panic on

picture day because your hair wasn't done and you couldn't find clean clothes to wear? Or was it the cruel, unrelenting teasing at school, with kids calling you a "bum" and laughing at you? Maybe it was that chubby little punk punching you in the stomach just because he didn't like you.

Or perhaps it was your boy cousins joking about the large mole on the tip of your nose before the surgery, calling you "Mo Mo" and chipping away at your already fragile self-esteem.

There was so much going on back then, it could have been any of the devastating situations that had taken place, and it almost broke you. But it didn't. You're still here. You made it through.

And now, just a few years later, here you are—spending the day with your best friend, Michelle Chambers, your Ace. The two of you skipped school today, hanging out at the playground, swinging back and forth, talking about tomorrow: the big move.

It's January 1983. It's freezing cold, just a few days before your thirteenth birthday, and skipping school feels like one last act of rebellion before everything changes. In your mind, this move feels like leaving Earth for another planet.

You're convinced it's the last time you'll have Michelle close by. But trust me, it's not. In just a few months, you'll be back together again, getting into new adventures and building a reputation in the projects on the Lakefront.

I know you're scared. Michelle tried to prepare you today, didn't she? Telling you all the horror stories she's heard about the projects. "If a boy asks you to be his girlfriend, you can't say no. He'll beat you up if you do," she said, her voice low and her eyes wide with fear. You sat there, the swing chains creaking, your heart pounding, trying to make sense of it all.

Let me tell you something: this move is a good thing, and it's going to change your life in ways you can't imagine. I know it's hard to believe that right now, especially after everything Michelle said. But trust me—I know. I'm you, just a few decades further down the road.

You were born on the South Side of Chicago, in the Woodlawn neighborhood, during a time when the Black community was raising fists in pride, and soul music echoed through the streets. While others fought for justice, you were learning what it meant to be po'—so poor you couldn't even afford the extra "o" and "r."

The kids at school didn't make things any easier. They thought you were weird, and you became their target. You cried often because their teasing cut deeper than you could explain. Remember how they'd yell, "I got the dirty touch!" if one of them accidentally brushed against you, as if your poverty was contagious? You were only seven years old, too young to understand why they treated you that way.

Mama did her best. "Forget them," she'd say, wiping your tears. For a moment, in her arms, you'd feel better. But the next day, it all started again.

And then you met Michelle Chambers, just a few months after that dark moment in your life. She was the first person who really saw you for who you were. Before her, you were just the awkward, skinny kid everyone avoided. The teasing, the fights, the bullying—it all weighed on you. But Michelle saw past all of that and became your lifeline.

The move to the projects sounds like a nightmare right now, but it's going to be the place where you begin to find yourself. Yes, there will still be struggles, but you'll also find acceptance and strength in ways you never expected.

Here's what you need to know: the teasing wasn't about you. It wasn't your fault. It wasn't because something was wrong with you. You carried that shame for so long, believing you deserved it, but you'll learn soon enough that none of it was true.

You'll shed that shame, piece by piece. The move, as scary as it feels, will teach you resilience. You'll discover the strength that's always been inside you, waiting to shine.

So, hang in there, young queen. The best is yet to come.

With love, You

Four

As a kid in the early 80s and growing up on the 66th block of Kimbark Avenue in Woodlawn, life was a constant balancing act between comfort and fear. When I was with the kids in my apartment building, things felt different. In that rundown, dilapidated building, surrounded by children who lived just like me, I wasn't the outcast. I was somebody.

Maybe it was because we all shared the same economic struggles, though none of us were old enough to understand what that really meant. We didn't need to. We just knew we were all in the same boat.

At home, I was respected in a way I never was at school. The younger kids in the building looked up to me, even though I didn't see myself as any kind of leader. I think it had something to do with the fact that inside those walls, we were all equals. No one teased me for being poor, or for the way I looked, or the things I didn't have. We were all navigating similar broken environments.

Where we lived was far from a safe haven, though. My mother moved us to places she could afford, stretching public aid that barely hit $400 a month in both cash and food stamps. Somehow, she managed to provide for me and my baby brother, struggling to make sure we had enough to get by. It wasn't easy, and there were days we went without.

She was brave and resilient, so much stronger than I realized back then. Getting the courage to ask her sisters for handouts, borrowing money she had no actual way of paying back just to take care of us. She took whatever life handed her and made it work, even when there wasn't much to work with.

In the three-story building we lived in, the broken entry doors were always open, welcoming stray cats and dogs that claimed the hallways as their territory. The smell hit you before anything else—animal urine and feces mingled with the sour tang of mildew and the heavy musk of hard living. It was the kind of stench that burrowed into your nostrils and lived on in your memories.

The communal bathrooms on each floor weren't used only by the tenants who paid rent. Folks from the street who knew the doors were always broken came in to use them, too. Every trip I made to the bathroom felt like a roll of the dice. Most of the time, they were filthy, except for a couple where tenants had installed locks to keep vagrants out.

Winters made everything worse. The freezing air mixed with the building's trapped heat and the overwhelming stench, creating an oppressive atmosphere that felt stifling—until you could retreat into the relative comfort of your own apartment.

The people in the building were a mix: single men and women, single mothers, a single father, and even an old man whose niece moved into his tiny one-room apartment with her five young children. Then there was the building's owners, an older married couple who lived on the entire first floor along with their adult children. Unlike the rest of us, their apartment had its own private bathrooms.

Somehow, we were a community—a messy, dysfunctional one, but a community nonetheless. We looked out for each other in small ways. But the perpetually unlocked front doors meant strangers wandered in regularly, using the bathrooms for whatever they needed: getting high, having sex, or finding a place to sleep. They left behind messes that rarely got cleaned —unless someone brave enough tackled the job, which wasn't often.

Inside our tiny two-room studio apartment on the second floor, we made do. The living room doubled as my mother's bedroom, where she slept with my baby brother beside her in a small crib. Her full-size bed took up most of the space, but she squeezed in a couch and a glass cocktail table—those were all the rage in the 80s. Across from the couch sat a component stereo system with a built-in 8-track player, a small luxury in an otherwise bare-bones existence.

The second room served as the kitchen, dining room, and my bedroom all rolled into one. That's where I slept—my twin bed tucked into the corner between the stove and a large front-facing window. Some nights, I'd stare out that window, looking at the stars and wondering what else was out there and imagining it had to be better than where I was.

But as comforting as that window could be, nights were also terrifying. I hated waking up in the middle of the night needing to use the bathroom. The fear of who might be in the hallway kept me from venturing out. There were times we'd pee in a bucket and pour it down the kitchen sink rather than risk going into those bathrooms.

Like the building's entry doors, the door to our apartment never locked properly—after it had been kicked in by one of Mama's exes, who didn't know how to take "it's over" for an answer. Instead of fixing the lock, the landlord left it, probably because they were as broke as we were. We made do by propping a chair under the doorknob to keep it closed at night. Sometimes we wedged a two-by-four up against it for good measure.

It was a crazy way to live, but we did what we had to. Mama was unemployed, raising us on welfare and trying to figure everything out on her own. No one ever talked to her about breaking the cycle of generational trauma.

No one taught her about credit, about financial planning, or how much harder things would be as a Black woman without a high school diploma, especially in the 70s and 80s. On top of everything, she had epilepsy, and though it was somewhat controlled with daily meds, it added another layer of struggle.

As a kid, I didn't know any better. I thought that was just life. It wasn't until I went to other family member's houses that I realized things could be different. They had locks on their doors. They had bathrooms inside their apartments. It was like another world.

Honestly, the biggest thing on my mind back then wasn't where we lived—it was the bullying at school. The teasing. The constant feeling that I didn't belong. I'm grateful that the kids in our building never treated me that way. Maybe it was because I was the oldest, or maybe it was because we were all in the same boat, but they looked up to me.

I'd organize the younger girls into cheerleading squads or rally everyone for jump rope competitions. Even the boys would jump in sometimes, showing off their double-dutch skills and often outshining the girls. It wasn't just a way to entertain ourselves or the neighborhood—it gave me something I didn't have anywhere else: a sense of belonging.

This was the side of me that Mama saw—the girl who got good grades in school despite the chaos there, who had a natural talent for writing and had a penchant to lead. To her, I was the world's greatest child. But no matter how much she believed in me, it wasn't enough to drown out the voices of the kids at school. What they thought of me mattered for some reason, and it ate away at me.

Even when we moved to the projects, and I found a new school where the kids were more accepting, I still couldn't shake the shame I carried with me, like Linus from Peanuts carrying his blanket. It wasn't just because of the bullying and teasing, though. There were other things that haunted me— things that had happened before I even turned seven. I didn't know how to process them, didn't know how to talk about them.

I thought the bad things that happened to me were my fault. That's why I could never bring myself to tell my mother—I was terrified she'd blame me, too. Later, when I got older and realized she'd never do that, I still remained silent. By then, my fear had shifted; I was afraid she'd blame herself, and I couldn't bear to put that burden on her. So, I kept it all inside, locked away, where it stayed for years.

Izora Davis was tough as nails. She ruled her house with a heavy fist, and yes, I feared her. She'd whip ass first and ask questions later, with no hesitation. And that look she'd give when she was not pleased? It was classic. It could stop you mid-sentence. Her face would harden like stone, and her eyes would flash with that "don't test me" glare.

No words were needed—you just knew. That toughness got her through the hard world we lived in, but it also built a wall between us. It kept me from opening up, from telling her about the things I was dealing with.

Some moments are still fresh in my memory, like they happened yesterday. That's the thing about trauma—it doesn't just go away. It stays with you. The difference now is that I can look back and see how those experiences shaped me. They gave me the strength to face challenges in my adult life that could have destroyed me otherwise.

I know how easily I could've fallen into a life of drugs, abuse, or worse, given how constantly I was exposed to those elements. But I didn't—and that's because of the strength I inherited from my mother.

I realize now how deeply connected my childhood struggles were to what Mama was going through at the time. The abuse she endured spilled over into our lives, touching everything. The dysfunction, the chaos—it wasn't just ours to bear. It was the ripple effect of the battles she was fighting every single day.

This next chapter delves into the hardships of my early childhood but also into the resilience that grew from it. Those experiences didn't just teach me how to survive—they gave me the foundation to rise.

Five

Mama had a thing for pretty boys. Or so I've been told. My father was one of them. I don't remember him, but the few black-and-white photos I've seen show a man with smooth, dark skin, deep waves in his hair, and a beautiful smile wide enough to earn him the nickname "Happy."

Mama used to say he could sing like a bird and reminded her of Nat King Cole. Being a sucker for a good crooner, she fell for him fast and hard when they met in 1969. I was born not long after. She was seventeen when she got pregnant, and she gave birth just six weeks after her eighteenth birthday.

A few months later, my father was killed. To this day, I don't know the details of what happened. What I do know is that Mama was left to navigate the world alone, with me—a newborn—in a time when single mothers didn't get much kindness or support.

According to her, my grandfather didn't make things any easier. When she told him she was keeping me, he threatened,

"I'll flush that goddamn baby down the toilet." So, with no other choice, she struck out on her own.

Parents back then often said wild things out of anger when their kids went against their wishes. But that same man—so big, so militant—would later love me like crazy.

But at that time, his words were taken as law. Mama was barely out of her teens, already dealing with the trauma of losing her first love and thrust into navigating an adult world on her own. How could someone that young be expected to handle all of that, let alone raise a child?

As fate would have it, by the time I was twenty-one, I had already repeated some of her cycles. Except by then, I had three children. I realize now why she was so disappointed when she first learned I was pregnant, and it wasn't only because I was having a child as a teenager. She was mortified that I was repeating her cycles, getting ensnared in the traps she hoped I would avoid.

Mama was fierce, strong, and unbreakable in her way. I know this from the stories I heard about her and from witnessing her strength firsthand. Even as a kid, she had a way of standing up for others, often at her own expense.

She butted heads with my grandfather, a stubborn, Southern-born WWII veteran who brought his family to Chicago in the 1950s. But she couldn't help herself—she was the protector, the one who spoke up, whether it was on her own behalf or for her siblings. That strength, though, didn't protect her from everything.

Not long after my father's death, Mama met another man. She was twenty, still too young to know any better, and he was older, smoother, with the looks of a god and the street smarts of a hustler. This man—let's call him Ro to protect his identity—was the most beautiful man on the South Side of Chicago.

He had gray eyes that sparkled when he smiled, and dimples so deep they looked like they could swallow him whole. Mama fell hard. He took her young toddler in as if I were his own, and until I was eight, when I met my paternal grandmother, I thought he was my father.

He cared for me and was my protector. I realize now just how much they both shielded me from the ugly realities around us. After he was gone, the things that happened in his absence proved that his protection had only been extended to me. His presence, however, was often a double-edged sword for my mother, bringing chaos as much as comfort.

Mama suffered under the weight of his flaws, and while I saw him as "Daddy," her family knew the hustler he truly was—a pimp, thief, drug addict, and woman-beater.

Mama refused to listen to their warnings. To her, Ro was who she wanted him to be. She was young, blinded by her idea of love. It wasn't until later, when she was trapped, that she admitted to me she hadn't believed he was a pimp until it was too late. By then, she was in too deep and leaving him wasn't as simple as walking away.

My earliest memories of him are from when we lived in the Wedgewood Towers, an old hotel converted into cheap apartments in Woodlawn. The place had a faded glamour, a remnant of a better past; however, by 1974, when we lived there, it housed mainly those struggling to survive—pimps, addicts, and the homeless. That building, with its chipped paint and cold hallways, became my first unwitting introduction to breaking and entering.

Mama and I were inseparable at the time. She taught me how to count, spell, and introduced me to the joys of reading. She read every single fable and all the fairy tales ever written. She never, ever denied me the opportunity to hear the story of Goldilocks and the Three Bears, Three Billy Goats Gruff, or the Three Little Pigs, even if I wanted to hear those stories every night. She told me how pretty the tooth fairy was whenever she brought me a shiny dime, placing it under my pillow after she took my tooth.

Occasionally she would leave me in Ro's care when she left the house. I was a sharp four-year-old, curious and clever. I was also nosy and had earned the name "Motor Mouth" with good cause. Basically put, I talked too much. When I saw Ro tiptoeing down the quiet long hallway and placing his ear against several doors, presumably listening for the neighbors, I was intrigued and wanted to do it too. "Daddy, I wanna hear!" I squealed to his horror, as he didn't realize I'd followed behind him.

He tried to no avail to shoo me back to the house and, appearing to be limited on time, gave up and made me his lookout while he jimmied the lock on one of the doors. When the door popped open, my sole job was to tell him if anyone got off the elevator, while he went inside and rummaged through the neighbor's things for something worth taking.

I thought we were on an exciting adventure. I followed him inside, and this made him move faster. When he opened the freezer, my eyes bucked at the box of ice cream bars, and I pointed and squealed with joy. Ro grabbed them. As he went from room to room, I saw Chapstick sitting among other random items on a cocktail table, and I picked it up. "Daddy, can I have this?" It didn't feel like stealing; it felt like a game.

Once we left the apartment and made it back into our own, Ro made me promise if anyone asked where I got my spoils to say, "My daddy bought it from the store." He coached me over and over until it was almost ingrained in my brain.

Later that day, as I was licking the vanilla ice cream on both sides of the frozen treat, my mother asked where it came from. I gave her a wide snaggle-toothed grin and in between licks, I gleefully replied, "My daddy got it out of that man's house down the hall."

That didn't sit too well with my mother, who didn't appreciate her baby being an accessory to robbery. Ro was upset with me because I forgot the script!

As crazy as it sounds now, this was what family meant to me. I had my mommy and daddy, and I believed with all my heart that they both loved and protected me. Sure, Ro had his flaws —robbing our neighbor wasn't exactly heroic—but in my young eyes, he was everything a father should be. My hero. My protector. I didn't see any cracks in the foundation they built.

Those cracks split wide open the first time I saw him brutally beat mama. Up until that moment, Ro was the man who I thought could do no wrong. But when I watched him raise his fists against Mama, that illusion shattered. It was like watching a superhero turn into a villain right in front of my eyes.

That night, everything changed. The man I trusted, the one I thought would always protect us, became the one I was suddenly afraid of. It was the first time I learned that love and fear can exist in the same space, twisting together in ways a child should never have to understand.

We moved a lot, but always within the Woodlawn community. Shortly after I turned six, we relocated to a building not too far away. At this point, mama took me with her everywhere, even late at night when I should have been in bed. She had no choice, especially after I told her what I saw one day while she was out.

A group of Ro's friends came to our apartment when mama wasn't home. I noticed they spent most of their time in and out of the small bathroom. While lying on the couch watching cartoons on a small black-and-white TV, out of the corner of my eye I could see one of his friends sitting on the lid of the toilet seat.

I turned in her direction, and our eyes met. Hers were glassy and subdued, and her arm was outstretched on top of the sink with a rubber strip tied tightly around it. Then her eyes rolled, and she leaned her head back.

I didn't understand what was happening, but she looked sick. Because it scared me, I told my mother when she came home. She yelled at Ro for "having junkies in the house gettin' high" around her baby. He yelled in response, "Don't worry about it; ain't nobody hurtin' Mimi!"

Ro didn't like being challenged. That night, after Mama threw his friends out, he came back, pounding on the door, screaming for her to let him in. I'd never heard him so angry. The door rattled with each blow, and I clutched my blanket, terrified.

Mama was sitting at a small table in the tiny kitchen, casually smoking a cigarette, when the door came crashing open. I screamed and jumped to my feet on the bed as Ro pushed his way through the mangled wood. Mama rushed out of the kitchen, and I ran into her arms.

He looked like a monster from one of the fairy tales Mama used to tell me—only this time, the monster wasn't trapped in a book. It was real, standing in our tiny apartment, veins bulging in his neck, sweat pouring down his face like he had just run a marathon. His furious eyes locked onto us as he yelled at her to put me down. The sound of his voice boomed throughout the apartment, and my heart pounded in terror.

Mama tried to keep her composure, pleading with him to leave as she held on to me. He refused, and as their screams collided, I couldn't move. All I could do was cry as I watched the two people I loved—the ones who made my little world feel complete—turn on each other.

And then, like the dark twist in a fairy tale where the damsel can't outrun the beast, came the fists.

The room turned into chaos as I ran and jumped behind the couch at my mother's command. His fists moved fast, each blow loud and violent. It sounded like thunder clapping over and over again. The monster wasn't just in the room—it had taken over the man I thought I knew, the man who was supposed to keep us safe.

The fairy tales Mama used to tell me always ended with the hero defeating the monster. But sometimes the monsters aren't hiding in the woods or lurking under the bed—they're standing right in front of you, and they look like someone you love.

I stood in the background, crying and begging for him to leave my mother alone. She was just as tough as him and, for a while, went toe to toe with him.

She was all of five-foot-two but packed a hefty 200+ pounds. For every punch he threw, she countered. Then he went into the kitchen and grabbed a pair of huge silver pliers, smacking her in the jaw with brute force. A loud cracking noise was quickly stifled by her tortured outcry.

I screamed, fearing he had killed her when she fell over on the bed. "Mimi, go get the landlord," I heard her screech, and I immediately ran toward the door.

Ro jumped at me quickly, blocking my way. "Mimi, sit yo' ass down! Your mama will be alright," he snapped, his chest heaving up and down as he still wielded the pliers in his hand.

I glared at him defiantly, refusing to obey.

"Girl, get yo' ass over there and sit down!" he yelled when I continued to stand my ground.

"Leave her alone, dammit!" my mother screamed, wincing from the pain.

"Tell her to go in the kitchen," he snarled, shaking the pliers in my direction.

"Baby, go on in the kitchen," she told me, the desperation in her voice resigned to the fear of his state of mind.

I ran back to the couch to get out of the way, but I wasn't going to the kitchen. I refused to go where I couldn't see mama. The fight continued. She overpowered him temporarily and yelled for me to get the landlord while she held him down. Still fearing for her, I ran out of the house and down to the landlord's apartment on the first floor. I frantically banged on her door, crying and begging her to help when she opened it.

The landlord, who was also the owner of the building, was surprised to see me and even more surprised when I relayed the details of what was going on. A middle-aged Black woman who lived alone, she was in her nightgown with pink sponge hair rollers pinning her hair.

She immediately she grabbed her keys and retrieved a pistol from another room, then told me to stay behind her as we ran up the stairs. When we reached the top, we could hear the fight still going on. The landlord entered the apartment and screamed for Ro to let my mother go.

"Get yo' old ass outta here! This ain't yo' business," he yelled as he struggled to hold mama down.

"It is my business; this is my place you tearin' up. Now get yo' ass outta here, nigga!" The older woman pulled the pistol out of the pocket of her nightgown and pointed it at him.

He stopped and looked at her like she had sprouted a second head. Then he stood up, and in his stupor, began arguing with her.

I ran into my mother's arms, clutching her as tightly as I could while Ro and the landlord yelled. Her face was swollen, a deep purple bruise already forming where the pliers had struck her. I could feel her body trembling as she yelled for Ro to leave. The landlord gripped the pistol as he inched closer, her voice sharp and commanding as she demanded that he stay back.

Ro wasn't having it—two women telling him what to do. He grabbed for the gun, his hand clamping around the landlord's wrist like a vice. Everything from that point happened in a blur. The room felt like it was closing in, every noise amplified —the scuffle of feet on the floor, the ragged breaths of my mother as she screamed at Ro, my own heartbeat pounding in my ears. I held onto Mama, burying my face in her chest as Ro and the landlady struggled over the gun.

Then it happened. The gun went off with a deafening bang that echoed through the small apartment. I screamed and my mother's arms tightened around me, shielding me instinctively. For a moment, everything went still, the chaos frozen in place like a scene in a movie. Then Ro took off running. The landlord let out a shaky breath as I cried uncontrollably.

"Nobody got hit," the landlord said, her voice breaking the silence as she pointed to the hole in the wall where the bullet had lodged.

A neighbor, disturbed by the sound of the gunshot, had called the police. After they arrived and took down the report, the landlord stayed behind, her stern face softening just a little as she looked at my mother. "Girl, this man is going to kill you," she said, not mincing any words as mama held me. "You have a little girl here. She's scared out of her mind. This has to stop."

Mama nodded, her swollen face cast downward, but she didn't say a word. As I looked up at her, I could tell she was trying to hold it together because she attempted to smile at me, then kissed me on the forehead.

The landlord sat down beside us and reached out, placing a hand on Mama's knee. "I'm telling you, if I see him around here again, I'm calling the cops, and I'll have him locked up. You have to think about this baby, not just yourself. Hell, she could have been hurt. I coulda been killed if the son of a bitch had gotten to my gun!"

I didn't know what Mama was feeling in that moment—whether it was shame or exhaustion. And even though I didn't understand everything they were talking about at the time, I could feel the weight of it settling in the room, as if some part of our lives had reached a breaking point.

Mama tried in vain to get me to go to sleep, but with all the madness that had taken place, there was no way I could close my eyes. She refused to go to the hospital for her injuries, and worse, she refused to press charges.

"Well, I don't know why you won't press charges against the bastard," the landlord continued. "But I tell you this: if I find out you let him back in, I'm gonna put you out."

Mama promised the landlord and me he wouldn't be coming back. But, as most abused women do, she reneged. He came back around selling dreams of us being a family and begging for forgiveness. She was easy to convince, and I was even more gullible. I wanted the man who I knew as daddy and her to be okay again. And she wanted what she thought was a family back together.

How could she, a young woman thrust into adulthood before she even finished her youth, know at the time how the decisions she made would not only affect her, but how they would impact me later in life? That witnessing this and similar relationship patterns would teach me this behavior was normal.

I grew up believing that if you loved someone, you were supposed to stick by them through anything—even if they were hurting you, even if they were breaking your spirit. It wasn't just her experiences that taught me this; she had grown up in a family where that belief was ingrained. Learning when to walk away wasn't easy for her, and it wasn't easy for me either. It was a lesson we both had to learn later in life.

After she would sneak him back into the apartment under the landlord's nose, our lives spiraled even more out of control. Mama found out the hard way; abuse does not go away simply because the abuser promises it will, especially when there are other underlying issues that trigger the abuse.

I used to wonder why many of these memories remained so fresh in my mind, as if they took place a few years ago instead of decades. The only explanation I can find is trauma.

Research shows that traumatic experiences can leave a lasting imprint on the brain. According to the National Child Traumatic Stress Network (NCTSN), childhood trauma alters the way the brain processes and stores memories, often making those events feel vivid and unforgettable, even years later.

The overall impact of these events was so significant that recalling them feels effortless. But that's the nature of trauma —it doesn't just fade away. It embeds itself, shaping how you think, feel, and respond to the world around you.

Some events, because I was too young to fully understand, I had to piece together when I got older. That knowledge made the memories even more traumatic, because it highlighted the true hell my mother was living.

I was unaware of everything Ro put my mother through, including how he used her to hustle to support his habit. She and I never talked about it, even when I faced my own struggles as a young adult living with an addict. Maybe she was ashamed, or maybe she had to push it out of her mind for the sake of her sanity.

I've learned that's what we sometimes do when the memories are too painful to confront. The abuse she endured with Ro only grew worse as time went on, but thankfully, she eventually found the strength and the will to leave him for good.

Even that moment was fraught with dysfunction as two of her sisters woke me out of my sleep early one morning. The oldest of my aunts was a levelheaded woman who kept the family grounded. Her patience, understanding, and caring nature were magnetic as it drew everyone together and bonded us all as a unit.

"Mimi, get up, baby. Come on, put your clothes on," she said sweetly that morning, as she pulled a shirt down over my head.

I was excited to see my family, but I was also confused.

"Where's my mama?" I asked, while getting dressed.

"She's okay, baby. Come on, let's go."

Something told me she wasn't being completely truthful. The anger on her face that betrayed the nurture in her voice was one clue; the questions my other aunt began asking was another.

Unlike the levelheaded sibling, my middle aunt was mama's emotional twin. She cussed like a sailor and would fight anyone at the drop of a hat.

"Did he touch you?" she demanded to know.

"Who?" I asked as my arms were being shoved into a long-sleeve shirt.

"That nigga! Did he touch you?" She grabbed my shoulders and looked into my eyes sharply.

I assumed she wanted to know if Ro whipped me, and I said no, which was the truth. Other than that crazy day, when he threatened me with the pliers, he never laid a hand on me. As we left the apartment without locking the doors, I asked where we were going and was told I was being taken away to be safe. I didn't know what that meant, but I didn't need to know. I was going with my aunts, which meant good food, the best desserts, and hanging with my cousins.

I was taken to my grandparents' house for a few days. Because no one would tell me what was going on and I was too afraid to keep asking (you didn't question adults in my day), I had to sneak and listen in on the conversations, from which I learned

41

a lot of new cuss words but got a vague understanding of what happened.

There was a lot of talk about me being taken away from my mother because of Ro. Hearing that saddened and frightened me. I knew my mother loved me more than anything in the world. Yes, there were many things going on that I was too young to understand, but she shielded me as much as she could. During this time, I never felt alone or sad. She looked out for me. And so did Ro.

Eventually, I learned that my mother had been incarcerated. She wanted me to stay with her friends, likely because she was still angry with my grandfather. Trying to honor her wishes, my grandparents reluctantly gave in. I was shuffled from house to house, moving between the people she trusted—or thought she could trust.

But here's the heartbreaking part: some of those so-called family friends, the same ones who judged my mother for being with Ro and accused him of hurting me, ended up doing far worse. They became the very people who put me in harm's way. In the process of being passed around, I was molested—not once, but twice.

This is one of those painful realities I did not have the heart to share with my mother—even when I became an adult. I didn't know how to tell her that in her absence, some of the people she trusted to take care of and protect me hurt me in unspeakable ways.

The first time was after I was taken to the home of a woman who looked down on my mother but smiled in her face. We called those people two-faced. Her opinion of me was just as nasty. I was treated like a dirty alley cat being brought in from the streets to be among her precious kittens.

I was six years old and already experiencing anxiety and stress because I was away from my mother, and I was being told that I was trash through the contempt of my host. I will never forget the way she looked at me and snapped, "You can't step foot in my kids' room until you've had a bath."

The derisive scowl made me wince, and her words felt like a slap across the face. She talked about my mother like a dog and said even worse about Ro. She thought her husband was the greatest thing on the planet and boasted my mother should have found someone like him. What she didn't know was that her husband, the man she labeled a saint, molested me when he was charged with bathing me while she was out.

I had never been touched by anyone the way he touched me. No matter how many drug addicts or other so-called misfits were in our lives before, no one had ever put a hand on me.

The giant of a man ran that bath his wife spoke of after he had been instructed to clean me up. He was about six feet tall with skin dark as tar and had a bald head. He always donned a foreboding countenance, a scowl that would frighten any child, even under normal circumstances.

When his wife left the house, he called me into the bathroom and closed the door as the water ran in the tub. Their children, all of them younger than me, must have had a clue to what was going on, because I could hear them snickering as they stood on the other side of the door.

He undressed me and asked if I had ever been touched "down there", pointing to my vagina. When I said no, the moments that followed scared me so that I trembled the rest of that night. He was very slow and deliberate, attempting to do with me things that should have only been done with a grown woman.

My screams of agony and the girls giggling and whispering "oooooh" on the other side of the door made him finally stop, but not before he tried unsuccessfully to penetrate my young body, bringing about a pain that would forever be seared in my mind.

The events that took place behind that closed bathroom door exposed me to the worse form of distress and confusion and set the stage for other terrifyingly similar events. I was traumatized because he hurt me and confused because I was supposedly in an environment that was touted as being safer than where I was before.

After he finally bathed me, he made me swear to secrecy. He warned that if I told anyone, I would be taken away from my mother forever. When I cried, he tried to soothe me with empty promises, saying he'd take me to see her the next day. Early the next morning, he repeated the threat, as if I needed reminding. But I didn't. The guilt and shame I carried from that night were more than enough to keep me silent. I only wish the memories had stayed sealed away, too.

I was relieved eventually to be reunited with my mother. I never opened my mouth about those incidents. Little did I know, they would not be the last times, but were the beginning of many painful episodes that I would shove into my bag of shame.

Six

I was overjoyed to see Mama when she was released. I had been waiting for that moment, longing for her comfort and the safety of her presence. But along with my joy, I carried a secret far too heavy for a child to bear. I couldn't forget the threat the scary man had made: if I told anyone what happened, I'd be taken away forever. The thought of being separated from her for good terrified me, so I stayed silent.

Like so many children who endure trauma, I did what I thought I had to do—I shoved it down, buried it deep, and tried to convince myself it hadn't happened. Studies show that over 60% of children who experience abuse never disclose it, often out of fear, shame, or a sense of responsibility for keeping their family intact. For me, that silence became my shield, but it also became my burden.

When Mama brought me home, she promised things would be different. And they were—at least for her. She came back with a new attitude, a new sense of freedom. At twenty-four, she was done with Ro and determined to take back her life.

She filled it with fun and laughter, throwing herself into parties, card games, and nights out with friends.

I loved watching her get ready to go out. Mama was truly a beautiful woman. She'd step out in colorful, tight-fitting pantsuits, platform boots, and bold Afro wigs that seemed to have personalities of their own. She looked like she was having the time of her life, and I loved seeing her happy. She deserved to be happy.

Because of the abuse I was becoming exposed to, things were different for me as well. Over the next year, it seemed as if I became a magnet for sexual deviants of all ages, each of them swearing me to secrecy with threats of having my mother locked up if the truth came out about what was happening to me.

Mama, oblivious to the storm I was weathering, was finding joy in her newfound independence. She partied at clubs, hosted lively card games at home, and surrounded herself with friends who seemed as colorful as her wardrobe.

While Mama didn't drink or do drugs, many of her friends did, dabbling in things I didn't fully understand at the time. They were an eclectic mix, each bringing their own quirks, dysfunctions, and stories into our lives. Some of them fascinated me, others scared me outright.

These people, labeled by society as misfits, became her tribe. No matter what they did—drugs, alcohol, living openly as gay or lesbian in a time when it wasn't widely accepted, or just being a little "off"—Mama welcomed them with open arms. She didn't judge them. Instead, she embraced them, becoming a source of strength for people who were often written off by the world. To them, she was a hero, and in their laughter and chaos, she found a sense of happiness that nothing else seemed to give her.

Not long after she had left Ro for good, she learned she was pregnant with his child. When my brother, Durelle, was born, my world changed in the best way. I was ecstatic to be a big sister. Even at seven years old, I took great pride in the role. I wasn't just his sister; I became his second caregiver.

Mama taught me how to feed him, burp him, and change his diapers, and I took to it naturally. On the nights when Mama went out to party, I treated him like one of my baby dolls, but with a love and devotion that only a big sister could feel.

Being Durelle's protector came naturally to me. He was my baby brother, and I loved him fiercely. I'd later get into plenty of fights because of him—because you could say and do what you wanted to me, but no one, and I mean no one, could hurt my baby. I took pride in looking out for him, always seeing myself as his shield.

But life has a way of flipping roles when you least expect it. For all the ways I thought I was protecting him, it was Durelle who saved me during one of the scariest nights of my life—and he was only a few months old.

Mama had gone out to party with her buddy, leaving me to look after Durelle. She trusted me—I'd proven myself responsible—but she didn't trust Ro. He'd been stalking her for over a year, trying to worm his way back into our lives. Mama was done with him, but he had a way of manipulating me.

Even though I hated him for what he did to her, a part of me was still daddy's little girl. I'd already made the mistake of letting him sweet-talk me into opening the door when Mama wasn't home. Because of that, she decided it was safer to leave

Durelle and me at her friend's apartment, just a few doors down from ours—somewhere Ro wouldn't think to look.

I don't know if it was because I was in a strange place, but I couldn't shake the fear that night. Durelle, only six months old, was sound asleep on the bed, completely unbothered. Meanwhile, I lay on the couch, trying to distract myself with The Carol Burnett Show and wishing Mama would come back early.

The apartment was too quiet, and that made it worse. Every little creak or shuffle of noise made my heart jump, like something bad was about to happen. My mind turned every sound into a monster or something hiding in the dark.

When a knock at the door shattered the silence, I froze. Did Ro find us? My heart pounded as I slid off the couch and tiptoed to the door, dragging a chair over so I could reach the peephole. My chest tightened at the thought of seeing Ro's face staring back at me. But when I peeked through the tiny hole, a wave of relief washed over me—it was Mama's friend's seventeen-year-old brother.

He had always been sweet to me, like a big brother. Whenever he came around, he'd bring me candy or slip me the spare change from his pockets. Seeing him at that moment made me feel like I could breathe again. I opened the door without hesitation and practically dragged him inside, my words tumbling out about how scared I was of being alone.

It didn't take long for me to notice that something was off. He was drunk. His words came out slurred, and he laughed too loudly at things that weren't funny. But even so, I was glad he was there. He was familiar, someone I trusted, and his presence made me feel a little less afraid.

He plopped down on the couch and turned on the television. "What's wrong, kid?" he asked, his voice slow and thick. He started talking to me about school, about little things that didn't matter, and for a while, I felt comforted. He invited me to sit next to him, and I didn't think twice. I climbed up onto the couch, grateful for the company.

When he put his arm around me, I felt safe. It was the kind of hug you'd expect from a big brother or a loving uncle, and I let myself relax. When he kissed me on the cheek, I giggled and pulled away shyly.

When he kissed my cheek again and I tried to pull away, he held my face in place, turning my head toward him, and then kissed me full on the lips. Having his lips on mine felt creepy and weird. When he tried to pry my mouth open with his tongue, I freaked out.

My heart pounded and a sick feeling came over me as my mind went back to that moment with the big, bad man in the bathroom. I tried pulling away again, but the more I struggled, the harder he pressed my face against his.

The smell of alcohol emanated from him, making my stomach turn. His words were slurred, but his grip was firm. When he finally let go of me, I made a run toward the bed where Durelle lay peacefully. But before I could reach it, his hand shot out and grabbed my arm, pulling me back.

"Where you goin', lil' mama?" he mumbled, his voice thick with drunken amusement. His glassy eyes looked me up and down as he patted his thighs. "Come and sit on uncle's lap."

Fear washed over me as I shook my head and tried to pull away. "No, I just wanna lay down with my brother," I said, my voice barely above a whisper.

But he wouldn't let me go. "C'mon now," he insisted, his tone still playful but laced with something that made my skin crawl. "It's just me. Don't be like that."

I resisted, my little body trembling. I had learned what it meant when boys wanted me to sit on their laps. I knew that "uncle" was just a word, a disguise for intentions I didn't fully understand but knew enough to fear. "No," I whispered, my voice cracking, "I just wanna go lie down."

His grip tightened, and then the panic kicked in. He pulled me down on the couch and tried to kiss me again. I struggled even harder to get away.

"What's wrong, Mimi? You don't like kissing?"

I shook my head emphatically.

"Don't you got a boyfriend?"

I shook my head again, while wishing mama would hurry and come back.

"Can I be your boyfriend?" he asked, kissing my cheek again.

I didn't know what to do or say, so I said nothing. When he laid me down on the couch and got on top of me, I cried out loud. The painful bathroom experience kept flashing in my mind, and I knew what was coming next. I closed my eyes and instinctively crossed my legs tight, praying hard for him to go away.

He kissed my eyelids, pleading with me not to be sad and promising he wouldn't hurt me. I knew better. Before I could protest further, he lifted off me and pulled my nightgown up over my head in two swift motions. The cold air hit my undeveloped body, and I threw my hands over my chest.

When I tried to scream, he covered my mouth with his hand, shushing me as he said he wanted to show me something. I remained quiet, trembling from fear and the cold air. Moving quickly, he lay on me again, placing my hands above my head and locking them there. Dread washed over me as he covered my mouth with his. Fresh tears sprang from my eyes while I begged God to make him stop.

He consoled me, constantly telling me not to be afraid and to trust him. He continually promised he wouldn't hurt me as he maneuvered himself to the lower extremity of my body. When I felt the coldness of his mouth touch my vagina, a frightened chill surged through my body, and I screamed and kicked until he fell over on the floor.

I jumped off the couch and ran toward the bed, crying uncontrollably and begging him to leave me alone. He angrily yelled at me to get back over to him. Then he swiftly removed his belt and started swinging it wildly at me, whipping me like I was his child.

He only stopped when I jumped on the bed, grabbed Durelle, and held my baby brother in front of me to discourage him from hitting me again. The sight of the baby's little body squirming in my arms and crying from being awakened must have made the drunken teen come to his senses.

He slumped down on the couch, his demeanor suddenly changing. Tears spilled down his cheeks as he begged me not to tell anyone what had happened that night. His voice, slurred and desperate, cracked as he pleaded, "If you tell, I'll go to jail forever. And 'the people' will take you away from your mama."

That threat was my kryptonite. The thought of being taken away from Mama was unbearable. So, I did the only thing I knew to do—I promised him I'd keep this secret, as long as he left me alone.

When he finally stumbled out the door, I wasted no time. I swiftly put the chain on the door, making sure he couldn't get back in. I stayed awake the rest of the night until Mama and her friend came back. I never saw him again after that night, but his words and actions lingered, burned into my memory.

Like so many other painful moments, I tucked that night away in the mental safe where I kept all my secrets. I locked it up tight and pushed it deep, telling myself that if I didn't think about it, it couldn't hurt me.

Looking back, I wish I had told Mama about the abuse when it first happened—not just with him, but from others as well. I wish I had trusted her enough to share what I was going through. But I didn't. I was too scared—of the repercussions, of being taken away, of the chaos it might bring.

Mama, in her own way, was trying to prepare me for independence, teaching me to stand on my own. But she didn't know what I was carrying. If she had, maybe she could have talked to me about sex and boundaries, about the ways people can harm you and the ways to protect yourself. Maybe she could have helped me understand that none of it was my fault.

Instead, I carried the weight alone, building walls to keep the pain out but also locking myself in with it. And though I vowed never to let it happen again, the scars of that night—and others like it—would stay with me for decades to come.

And it would happen again, despite my personal vows.

As a little girl, I didn't know my body was a beautiful and pure temple that wasn't supposed to be invaded by anyone. I didn't understand what was happening to me; I was being raped physically, defiled emotionally, and destroyed psychologically. Because of it all, I felt dirty and ashamed. Therefore, it was so easy for me to be affected by what others said and thought about me.

Those feelings I harbored for myself, as well as fear, are why I could not tell my mother, my family, or anyone else what was happening to me. I took responsibility for all of it—something no child should have to do. Not telling my mother or someone else was the biggest mistake I would ever make. Eventually, I would try to put it so far out of my mind that it would be like it never happened.

However, the mind has a way of bringing reality back to bite you. In trying to forget what I went through as a child, I opened the door for other dysfunctions to enter and settle into my life, not fully gauging why I equated sex with love and thought it normal to be abused while becoming a woman.

Had my mother been made aware, she could have helped me understand what was happening to me. I have no doubts if she knew, the first time would have been the last time. She would have told me it wasn't my fault. She would have fought for and protected me. She would have addressed the abusers and possibly stopped them from doing the same thing to other girls. I have no doubt those who molested me did the same to others.

These are just a handful of things I wish I could have talked to her about. As an adult, because so much time had passed, I didn't know how to tell her that my childhood was filled with so many traumatizing moments. It was no longer fear that bound my tongue; it was the impenetrable shame and guilt that taunted me, making me believe I should have known better. Of course, I know it was not my fault. At least, I know this now.

For most of my life, I didn't understand how molestation, rape, and being teased and bullied impacted my self-esteem and, eventually, my development as a woman. I was once advised, before my mother's untimely passing, that I needed to open up to her about my experiences and my pain. I could never bring myself to disclose those things to her.

As a mother myself, I know firsthand the level of guilt we take upon ourselves when something bad happens to our children. The thought of her lamenting over something that happened to me decades ago would only cause more pain.

So, I reconciled the guilt and shame within myself after acknowledging some important truths:

- I was not damaged goods.
- I was not a victim.
- I was a survivor.
- I didn't have control over the past, but I could limit its impact on my future.
- This is worth repeating: I could limit its impact on my future.
- Finally, I had to forgive myself.

When I leaped over that last hurdle, the undeserved resentment I held in my heart toward my mother for other non-related events was replaced with a love so powerful that it rocks my heart to this day. My world was shattered when she was taken away from us suddenly the day before her older brother's funeral. When the phone call I always dreaded would come, it ripped me apart.

Her presence is so strong, even in death. She left a powerful legacy that will not soon be forgotten. She grew by leaps and bounds as a woman and became a soldier for so many who didn't know how to fight for themselves. She made an impact on her grandchildren, who carry the trait of her strength. Most importantly, I am who I am because of her.

I have finally learned to not live with regrets. However, if there was one thing I could say to my mother that I never got to say before she departed this life, it would be this: I love her so much that the heavens can't contain it. I feel her with me every day, and I know she is watching, guiding, and teaching me. I admire the woman she became, and I respect the journey she walked in becoming that woman.

And I would thank her. She taught me how to survive. She showed me how to never give up. She helped me understand what it is to be a woman.

She is my shero!

Seven

As a little girl, my mother would help me go to sleep by reciting fairy tales. My hero was Little Red Riding Hood. I loved Red. She was brave, venturing into the woods on her own, carrying that basket of goodies for her grandmother. But what I admired most was how smart she was. She spotted the big bad wolf's disguise and outwitted him, saving herself.

The way Mama told the story, the wolf dressed up as Red's Granny and waited for Red in the bed. When Red arrived at the cottage, she knew something was off. She moved toward the bed slowly, suspicion nagging at her. "Granma, what big eyes you have," she said.

The wolf, using a sweet, high-pitched voice, replied, "The better to see you with, my Dear." Red kept pushing, calling out all the things that didn't look right until she got to, "Granma, what big teeth you have!" That's when the wolf dropped the act, growling, "The better to eat you with, my Dear!"

But Red didn't freeze. She ran. She trusted her instincts, and they saved her.

Wouldn't it be great if life worked like that? If we always listened to that voice inside telling us when something wasn't right? I didn't have that kind of foresight when I was younger. Most people don't. And honestly, that's not a judgment—it's just life.

My own experiences gave [1]me the awareness to shield my children from the things I didn't want them to see, feel, or go through—especially my daughters. I wanted better for them, a life untouched by the pain I had endured.

Growing up, I knew little about my mother's past aside from those things I witnessed firsthand. Like many women of her generation, she didn't talk about her abuse. It wasn't until I became an adult that I learned bits and pieces of her story. What I've come to understand about her journey has only deepened my respect for her strength. Still, I sometimes wonder—if I'd known her history earlier, would it have made a difference for me? Probably not.

The truth is, if something has a greater purpose in your life, fate will ensure you go through it—no matter how much you try to avoid it. My mother, or anyone else, could have walked me step by step through their struggles and told me exactly what not to do. But unless they followed up that advice with a crystal ball showing me the future, it likely wouldn't have prevented me from living through my own lessons.

Like Red, I had to venture out into the woods and discover life for myself. And life, as I learned, is full of wolves lying in wait,

---

1. https://www.cdc.gov/suicide/facts/data.html?utm_source=chatgpt.com
   https://www.cdc.gov/nchs/data/databriefs/db471.pdf?utm_source=chatgpt.com

disguised and ready to pounce the second you fall for the okey-doke. I can't tell you how many times I landed in a situation I knew, instinctively, I should've walked away from.

The hell I went through because I ignored that little voice inside? Let's just say it was enough to make me understand what my mother tried to protect me from. But life is not designed for you to follow a step-by-step guide. You learn as you go, and sometimes, you learn the hard way. And unfortunately, as Mama used to say, "A hard head makes a soft ass."

Although I didn't get to say goodbye, I'm grateful that, when she was alive, my mother saw me growing into the woman she had always hoped I'd become. In fact, I'm still growing. I often look to my past because it holds the answers to many of the dilemmas I face today and the key to unlocking my continuing success.

Reflecting on these painful memories reminds me of Little Red Riding Hood's journey through the woods. Facing the potential dangers along her travels and wolves lurking in disguise, navigating childhood trauma feels like stepping into a dense, dark forest.

You're a child, skipping along with your basket of hope and innocence, only to be ambushed by challenges you never saw coming. The wolves—be they bullying, abuse, or rejection—don't just hurt you in the moment. They leave scars that can take years to heal.

Just as Red trusted her instincts when she noticed something wasn't right with "Granny," I wish I'd had that same ability to trust my gut as a child. But when you're already dealing with trauma, like sexual assault, your instincts often feel muted by the noise of shame and fear. That's when the wolves strike hardest, exploiting your vulnerability. And, just like Red had to face the wolf alone, I often felt alone in my pain.

Too often, adults dismiss bullying as a phase—a rite of passage every kid has to endure. I think that's what some of my teachers believed back in the 70s. They rarely stepped in when bullying happened, even though it was blatant. But bullying isn't harmless banter, and it's definitely not a character-building exercise. For the child being targeted, it's rejection in its rawest form. It's a loud, persistent message: You don't belong. You're not enough. You'll never fit in.

The damage goes deeper than people realize. For bullied kids, the damage lingers long after the taunts end. Studies show that nearly 20% of U.S. students report being bullied at school, according to the National Center for Education Statistics. For many, the scars last a lifetime, shaping their self-worth and how they navigate the world as adults.

Bullying isn't just about the cruel words or actions—it's about what they make you believe about yourself. Each insult chips away at your confidence, until you start wondering if the lies they tell about you might actually be true. Like Red, initially standing there questioning the wolf's disguise, you doubt your instincts, even your sense of reality.

The effects are profound. A 2021 report by StopBullying.gov highlights that bullied children are more likely to struggle academically and socially. Their confidence takes a hit, their ability to trust becomes fragile, and they carry those wounds with them well into adulthood. It's not just a phase—it's a trauma, one that alters their sense of self and their place in the world.

As adults, it's easy to say, "Kids can be cruel," and move on. But for the child enduring it, bullying feels like a storm they can't escape. The teasing and humiliation pound against their sense of worth, leaving them desperate for shelter. Sure, the phase might end, but the aftermath—the devastation—can last a lifetime.

If left unchecked, that pain can push a child into dangerous places. Desperation often takes the form of cries for attention: skipping school, acting out, or turning to drugs or alcohol to dull the hurt. For some, the pain becomes so overwhelming that they seek permanent solutions to escape it. The level of anguish required to take that step is unimaginable. But I understand it—because I've been there.

It's only by the grace of God that I'm here to tell my story. I was so tired of being rejected and teased, of carrying the shame of being molested, that I tried to end my life when I was just nine years old. I was standing face-to-face with the wolf, feeling cornered, with no way out. My cries for help started as deep, gut-wrenching sobs, but eventually, they turned into a desperate plea for relief.

One day, in the middle of my misery, I wrote a suicide note. In a move that reflected both my pain and my need for someone to notice, I handed it to a classmate. That note traveled from one student to another, eventually landing on my teacher's desk.

Not knowing what else to do—bless his heart—the teacher sent me to the office. They called my mother, and someone at the school tried to talk to me about what was going on at home. But the conversation was surface-level at best. No one dug deep enough to uncover the wolves hiding in the woods.

To understand why, an otherwise smart and creative nine-year-old girl was threatening to un-alive herself. Instead, I was left feeling exposed, vulnerable, and more uncertain than ever.

The attention I'd drawn to myself fed the shame gnawing inside me as my embarrassment grew.

The kids who already teased me for being "dirty" now had new ammunition. They started calling me "crazy," piling on the insults with pointing and snickers. Their mocking was relentless, and every snide comment or cruel laugh expanded my bubble of awkwardness and shame until it felt ready to burst. It was like the wolf caught me, chided me for being weak, and I had no way of defending myself. I withdrew deeper, convinced that everything they said about me was true.

At that moment, I truly believed no one cared whether I lived or died. I was tired of crying, tired of feeling worthless, and I did not know how to process all the emotions clawing at me from the inside. In my mind, the only way to stop the wolf's attacks was to let it devour me. I scolded myself for writing that letter in class—it had been a mistake to show my vulnerability. Next time, I thought, I wouldn't announce my plans to the world. I would just do it.

I even knew how. A woman who lived in the same building as my grandparents had done it before.

My mother always had a ton of prescription pills—medications for her epilepsy and the headaches that followed each episode. Back then, I didn't know which pill did what. To me, they were just orange bottles in a large plastic bag, easily accessible. It was the 70s, before childproof caps were common. In that moment of desperation, I grabbed a few bottles, twisted off the lids, and swallowed a handful—just like the neighbor in my grandparents' building had done.

I don't remember much about the note I wrote beforehand, only that it was meant to explain my reasons. The rest is a blur. What I do remember is my cousin, Ozea, showing up. He probably came over that day just to check on me, but instead, he found me completely out of it—dazed, unsteady, and clearly not okay.

Ozea didn't waste a second. He called my mother immediately, and together, they helped me get the pills out of my system. I saw how much my cousin cared, how much it mattered to him to protect me when I couldn't protect myself. If he hadn't shown up, if he hadn't acted so quickly, I wouldn't be here to tell this story. I owe him my life. It's a debt I'll carry with gratitude forever.

Thankfully, that one and only attempt was unsuccessful. Had I taken the right pills or if my cousin hadn't recognized that something was wrong and acted quickly, my voice would have been silenced forever. But more than that, the lives of my children and grandchildren—their dreams, their legacies, their potential—would have never come into existence. That thought humbles me every time I reflect on it.

That night did something else, too—it opened my mother's eyes. She realized her little Red was in pain, carrying something far heavier in her basket than she could have ever imagined. I told her pieces of the truth, the parts I could bear to share. There were things I couldn't bring myself to say. Some pains felt too big, too overwhelming, to speak aloud.

I never told her about the times I was molested. I couldn't separate what had happened to me from who I thought I was. I still believed it was my fault, that somehow, I was to blame for the terrible acts perpetrated by sick men and boys. That shame was suffocating, and I carried it alone, too afraid of the fallout to speak the truth.

Unfortunately, this silence is common. According to the Rape, Abuse & Incest National Network (RAINN), about

93% of child sexual abuse victims know their abuser, and yet most never tell anyone at the time. The reasons are obvious—fear, shame, guilt—and the result is often the same: survivors grow up carrying an invisible weight that affects our mental health, relationships, and sense of self.

For me, that weight was paralyzing. The shame I felt wasn't just a byproduct of what happened—it became part of my identity. I carried it like armor, protecting myself by keeping everything locked away, but that same armor kept me from healing. It's a common experience for survivors of abuse.

Research confirms that childhood trauma, including sexual abuse, increases the risk of depression, anxiety, and even post-traumatic stress disorder (PTSD) in adulthood.

I see now how much that silence cost me. It kept me locked in a cycle of self-blame and guilt, unable to heal from what I hadn't even named. But even in that moment, even as I held so much back, my mother's concern affirmed something important: I wasn't alone. That knowledge, as small and fragile as it felt, was the first step toward understanding that my voice mattered, even if it would take years for me to use it fully.

What I did share with her was the torment I felt from all the teasing and bullying, and how it left me feeling like I didn't matter. She listened, pulled me close, and told me how special I was. Her words were like a balm, soothing in the moment, even if they couldn't take the pain away completely.

The rest of my older male cousins, just a few years ahead of me, stepped in to support me in their own way. They rallied around me, and since they went to the same school, they made a promise to protect me from the bullies. They didn't just stop there—they taught me how to fight, so I could defend myself.

It wasn't just about swinging fists; it was about helping me believe I didn't always have to shrink away or take what was being thrown at me. I made a solemn promise to my family and myself that I would never again attempt to take my own life. Tragically, many young people today find themselves in similar situations, and some do not survive.

Suicide remains a leading cause of death among adolescents. In 2021, it was the third leading cause of death for individuals aged 10 to 14 and the second for those aged 15 to 24. Between 2007 and 2021, suicide rates for people aged 10 to 24 increased significantly.

These statistics underscore just how crucial mental health support and intervention are for today's youth. The pain someone must be experiencing to take that step is unimaginable, to say the least. I cannot stress this enough: if you or someone you know—child or adult—is struggling, please find someone to talk to or something to help you cope with those overwhelming emotions. No one should have to bear that burden alone.

Eight

The Wiz wasn't just a televised iconic moment in the Black community. The dancing, the rhythm, the energy—it all captivated me. Watching my favorite singers and actors bring the story to life felt so magical. But what made it even more special was seeing characters who looked like me. For the first time, one of my favorite movies of all time (the original Wizard of Oz) felt personal, familiar, and relatable in a way that nothing else during that era had before.

And the music—oh, the music. It was like an extension of my soul. Every note, every beat, every lyric pulled me in and wrapped around me like a warm hug. The songs weren't just background noise; they were part of the journey, part of the struggle, and part of the triumph. It mirrored my life, in a way, because music had always been my refuge, my way of escaping the chaos around me.

Growing up, music was more than just entertainment for me —it was survival. Whenever life felt overwhelming, it became my sanctuary. Our home was filled with albums, records, and eight-track tapes, and I would play them late into the night until I drifted off to sleep.

The O'Jays, Prince, Michael Jackson, Rita Ward, Earth, Wind & Fire, Boston, Kool & the Gang, Elton John, The Brothers Johnson, and gospel music—all of it gave me a sense of peace and kept me grounded.

But the most special music didn't come from a record or the radio—it came from Mama. She had a beautiful voice. Some evenings, she'd sit on the front stoop with the neighborhood crooners, to doo-wop and R&B songs from the fifties and sixties. But the moments I loved the most were when she sang just for me.

Reminiscing on The Wiz, I see so much of my own story reflected at me. At a young age, I was trying to navigate a world that felt confusing and often frightening. I was always searching for something that seemed just out of reach— stability, belonging, security. Like Dorothy, I was just trying to find my way home, but home wasn't a place. It was a feeling, a sense of peace I hadn't yet discovered.

The need to find calm stemmed from the chaos raging inside of me because of the secrets I was carrying. Back then, I thought staying silent was my way of protecting Mama. I believed that by burying my most painful experiences, I was sparing her the burden of knowing what I'd been through— especially the times I'd been molested. Deep down, I also blamed myself, as if somehow I was at fault.

Years of growth and understanding gave me the opportunity to see the truth: my silence didn't protect anyone. It only deepened my wounds. It trapped me in a suffocating cycle of guilt and shame. By keeping everything inside, I wasn't just hiding my trauma—I was letting it control me.

Breaking free of that cycle became the fight of my life as an adult. I had to confront my fears, face the things I had buried, and trust that my heart was strong enough to handle it. But as a child, I had to find coping mechanisms to help me through it. Listening to music became my lifeline, loosening the grip of despair, the lyrics giving me the encouragement to keep moving forward. It didn't erase my pain, but it gave me a way to process it.

Over the years, just like Dorothy, I eventually realized that the power to change my life, to find my way home, had been with me all along. My version of clicking my heels wasn't a magical incantation—it was the slow, steady work of self-discovery and healing. It was finding the courage to face my past and the strength to believe in my future.

Even now, music is still my haven. My husband loves to tease me about knowing too many songs from as far back as the 50s, joking about seeing my birth certificate whenever I belt out a tune from decades past. But those songs aren't just nostalgia for me—they're my history, my comfort, my salvation.

Life will always have its tornados, its witches, and its wolves in disguise. It will try to knock you down, make you question your worth, and convince you that you're not enough. But if there's one thing I've learned, it's that you're stronger than you think. Everything you need to heal, to grow, to find peace—it's already inside you.

The Tin Man thought he didn't have a heart, but he did. And it was full of love. The Cowardly Lion thought he'd be afraid forever. But he found courage. The Scarecrow thought he didn't have the intelligence to be anything more than stuck on a stick. But he found his sense of self.

Dorothy thought she needed someone to guide her home, but she didn't. And neither did I. It took time, pain, and a lot of music, but I found my heart, my power, and myself. The ruby slippers weren't just a symbol—they were a reminder that the answers we seek are often right inside of us. We just have to believe.

Nine

As a teenager, even my secrets had secrets. By then, I had mastered the art of silence, tucking away my thoughts and feelings where no one could see them. On the outside, I started blending in more, following the patterns of my peers. But fitting in didn't always lead to the best decisions.

The innocence and pragmatism of youth has a way of making us think we have life all figured out and know what we're doing. Sadly, we confuse certain benchmarks in our lives as gateways for venturing into dynamics for which we are not prepared.

As my body began to change and I started developing an interest in boys, I followed my young and dumb instincts—ones that tripped me up every time. I believed that a boy's attention automatically meant I was compelled to have sex with him and at times I would confuse those quick moments with love. Those beliefs were misguided and left me vulnerable to making choices I wasn't ready to face.

Despite it all, I was still what most people would call a "good girl." I avoided trouble, studied hard, and did well in school. My mother had high hopes for me—she dreamed I'd go away to college, become a lawyer, and build a successful life. But little did she know, the weight of the secrets I was carrying would eventually bring all of those plans to an abrupt halt.

I was afraid to talk to my mother about sex. That fear was pretty normal for teens in the 80s, but my first attempt to edge into that kind of discussion came when I was only thirteen. A grown-ass man-child had convinced me he loved me. He claimed he was only 18 (still too old for me), and he told me I was "ready." And, of course, I believed him.

When I tried to bring the topic up to my mom, her initial response was exactly what you'd expect from a parent whose pre-teen even hints at an interest in sex. She nervously asked, "You're not having it already, are you?" I quickly put her at ease and told her no, which was the truth.

Then came her scolding, which was preceded by "the look": "Go sit your ass down somewhere!" That was the end of that conversation.

I often wonder what might have happened if I had opened up to her. If I had told her about the events that had shaped my life and admitted how confused I felt, and how much I needed her guidance. For any child, raising the topic of sex with a parent at such a young age is scary. For me, it felt like it would open the door to deeper, more challenging conversations.

Would she have been ready to confront my reality?

I wasn't yet sexually active, but thoughts about it lingered in my mind—not because I was prepared for that step. I didn't even know what it felt like to experience desire. It wasn't passion fueling my curiosity; it was the pressure from boys who bragged about their supposed conquests. According to them, I was the only one "holding out," and that made me feel like a fool.

When I liked someone, I thought I had to be ready to "put out" to keep their attention. Some of the boys' boasting was true—many girls in the neighborhood became pregnant before they even started high school.

My unresolved past and shaky self-esteem made me long for love too soon. I clung to the misguided belief that sex would make me into the adult I thought I wanted to be so bad. And the even bigger myth—that it would make my acne go away.

By the time we moved into the projects on Chicago's lakefront when I was thirteen, I had moved past being seen as a social misfit. Although I arrived in the south side community of Kenwood-Oakland with my self-esteem shattered, I wasn't treated like an outcast. I got along with most of the kids. The project community felt like one big family—everyone knew each other, and neighbors looked out for one another. Most of the kids attended the same schools, all within a one-mile radius.

Some of the girls who read the stories I wrote—I was a consummate writer, encouraged me to keep writing, and my teachers supported and celebrated my creativity. The bullying I had faced in my old community was behind me, though I occasionally found myself in fights with groups of girls.

This time, the conflicts were about their wandering boyfriends —boys whose attention I never reciprocated. It's funny how at even young ages, girls fight each other over boys instead of holding the boys accountable; but that's a discussion for another book.

The 80s were an interesting time, a revolutionary mix of innovation and cultural expression. Wide-leg pants gave way to the preppy look, and bold neon colors replaced psychedelic prints. Hairstyles like full-length gheri curls were all the rage, inspired by icons like Michael Jackson and Prince, who defined what was hot.

Music videos and dance trends, from breakdancing to the moonwalk, were staples of everyday life, and hip-hop was cementing its place in the culture. Block parties, boomboxes, and double-dutch were the heartbeat of the Black community, connecting everyone in the neighborhood.

In the hood, being labeled a gangbanger's "woman" was seen as a badge of honor. That title came with certain perks— protection, the opportunity to wear their gold chains or earrings, and the prestige of being associated with someone feared and respected.

But there were downsides too, like sharing that title with a "main chick" and often being one of many vying for attention. I never aspired to that role or the so-called benefits. In hindsight, my lack of interest in titles or lifestyles tied to gang culture made me a curiosity, a magnet for those who wanted to figure me out.

Still, while I was doing better socially, I was also incredibly green. When I turned fourteen, I let a smooth-talking gangbanger—who claimed to be sixteen—convince me to give him my precious virginity. I later discovered he was an adult, preying on quiet, naive girls like me.

One of the legendary myths about sex is the romanticized idea of the "first time." It's often portrayed as a starry-eyed event where two souls merge in a euphoric union, a magical moment of bonding and desire. But for many young girls, the reality is far from that dreamy narrative.

My first experience was painful and disillusioning, involving a liar with a notorious reputation for "breaking in" virgins. He was the physical embodiment of Red Riding Hood's wolf, lurking in the shadows, waiting to deceive naïve young girls and devour their innocence.

This wolf promised to "make me a woman." I liked the sound of that—the title, the concept. I was eager to leave behind girlhood, which I thought was for the birds. What I didn't understand was the depth of what it truly meant to be a woman, or how much I would someday yearn to reclaim those youthful years.

Here is the advice I wish someone had given me back then: "If you're thinking about sex, don't let anyone convince you it will make you a woman (or will get rid of your nature bumps). Becoming a woman has absolutely nothing to do with sex."

That's why I cringe when I hear a certain singer proclaim, "You may be young but you're ready ... you're not a little girl, you're a woman ..."

They called that first sexual experience 'breaking in', and that's exactly what it felt like. I wish I had been strong like Red and ran away from the big bad wolf when he displayed his fangs, announcing his intentions in that cold, dirty and dark vacant project apartment. Instead, I stayed and my virginity, and what was left of my innocence, was devoured.

I didn't experience the same sensations he did as he moaned in pleasure. I cried in pain, begging silently for the assault on my body to end. He promised the second time would be better, saying because he broke me in, it wouldn't hurt anymore. I didn't believe him, and I never allowed him to touch me again.

It wasn't easy quitting him, because you didn't break up with those kinds of guys. They ran through girls until they grew tired of them, tossing them away like garbage for the next one to pick up. This particular guy was also known for beating on his girlfriends.

I was terrified to tell him I wanted out. Although he had never shown aggression toward me, his reputation spoke for itself. That became all too real when one of his "women" confronted me, accusing me of sleeping with her man. I tried to explain that I did not know he was involved with anyone, but she wasn't interested in my excuses. The fight was set for later that night—whether or not I wanted to brawl—so she could gather her girls for my beat down.

That fight never happened. When I told him about her accusations and her threat to have me jumped, he told me not to worry. The next day, I braced myself for another confrontation when I saw her. Instead, she surprised me by apologizing. It wasn't her apology that shocked me, though— it was the swollen black eye she was sporting, one that hadn't been there the day before.

It didn't take a rocket scientist to figure out what had happened. I knew then that I had to get out, but the thought of telling him only deepened my fear. What would he do to me for trying to leave? Still, I knew I had to take the chance.

When I finally told him I couldn't stay in the relationship, using the excuse that I wasn't ready to have sex again, his reaction stunned me. He accepted my decision, even called me a "good girl." Relief washed over me, especially since I had expected the same violent treatment he'd dealt to his others.

This is the messiness a young lady venturing into adult situations finds herself in. I was completely out of my element, having been suckered in by the appeal of being liked and desired. Young girls in my age group seemed to revel in the drama, excelling early in the school of hard knocks. I stuck to my guns and didn't engage in sex again until I was sixteen. I was still too young, but by that time, I thought I knew what I was doing.

Everyone was doing it, and it was all that was being talked about. So, what was I waiting for? It was on television, in music, and on the mind of every boy and girl with whom I came in contact. Since it was so popular, I thought it must be okay and felt emboldened to give it another try.

One of the tricky things about being a teenager is how easily you can get caught up in what's popular. Whether it's sex, drinking, or drugs, the desire to fit in with the crowd that seems to be having all the fun can be overwhelming.

Some adults understood this and tried to step in. High schools started offering sex education as a form of prevention. They covered topics like different methods of birth control, the dangers of sexually transmitted diseases, and even showed videos about the pains of childbirth. But despite these efforts, they couldn't stop the teenage pregnancy epidemic of the time.

Teen pregnancy rates soared in the 1980s. By 1990, teen births peaked at 61.8 per 1,000 females aged 15–19, reflecting trends that had already been climbing throughout the late '80s. Programs back then struggled to address the deeper societal and emotional factors that drove teenage sexual activity, leaving many young girls unprepared for the consequences.

The videos shown during Sex Ed scared the hell out of me. They were enough to prompt me to work up the nerve to talk to my mother about sex again. At sixteen, I thought I was mature and ready for the world. I figured she'd be more receptive, especially if I told her I wanted to get on birth control. See how mature I was being? With so many girls in our community getting pregnant, I thought she'd be relieved that I wanted to protect myself.

"Are you fucking?" she challenged bluntly, glaring at me with her infamous evil eye.

Nothing had changed—Mama was still Mama. Out of that familiar sense of fear (my mother was a swinger in the literal sense—she could swing and hit with an accurate dexterity that made you think twice about saying the wrong thing), I said no. Only this time, it wasn't true. I was sexually active, and I had hoped we could have a real conversation about it, one that might lead to steps to protect me from pregnancy.

But I hadn't given her enough facts to make that kind of decision, so her response was the same as it always was: talk to her when I was ready. Instead of being honest about what was going on, I chickened out. I walked away, and I never broached the subject again.

I wish she had pressed me more, though. Maybe she was more afraid of the truth than I was afraid of her.

Although I often cooed and marveled over my teenage friends' babies, deep down, I was panicking. The idea of getting pregnant terrified me. If my period was even a day late, I'd spiral into a full-blown panic. Watching other girls struggle with babies and their endless baby daddy drama didn't stop me from wanting to have sex—it only fueled my determination not to get pregnant.

I decided to take fate into my own hands and went to the neighborhood clinic to get birth control on my own. But it wasn't that simple. I was told I needed parental consent or my parent's medical card. I knew my mother well—there was no way I could get her to come to the clinic without being completely honest, and I couldn't get access to her medical card. If I asked for it, I'd have to explain why I needed it. Rather than face her wrath or judgment, I let the matter go.

Back in the 80s, getting birth control as a teenager wasn't as accessible as it is now. Parental consent was often mandatory, and even clinics that claimed to be teen-friendly had barriers in place. Today, in many states, minors can access contraception confidentially through public health programs and initiatives like Title X.

The cultural shift toward recognizing the importance of accessible birth control for teens has helped reduce unintended pregnancies, but back then, those options weren't widely available—or widely known.

I thought I was adult enough to have sex, but I was still very much a child, afraid to talk to my mother about what I was doing. That fear and my avoidance of honest conversations would catch up with me.

In high school, I thrived academically during my first three years. As a sophomore, I earned a spot in the Principal Scholar's Program, and by junior year, I was inducted into the National Honor Society. I stayed busy and engaged, immersing myself in activities thanks to the encouragement of my history teacher, Ms. Ball, who recognized the talent within me. Teachers like her were treasures, and while other students found her annoying and mean, she was a god-send to me.

Under her influence, I embraced challenges I might have otherwise avoided. I joined the student council, took part in Know Your Heritage—a televised high school trivia competition hosted by the legendary LeVar Burton—and served as a youth lawyer in mock trials.

Ms. Ball's encouragement pushed me to compete in the Academic Olympics with just a day's notice, where I proudly secured third place. One of my most cherished achievements during this time was landing a coveted science internship at Wheaton College. That summer, I got to live in a dorm during the week, exploring new academic frontiers and experiencing independence for the first time.

My mother beamed with pride. Her baby girl had surpassed her own achievements in school and seemed to have a bright future ahead. It's what every parent hopes for—to see their children take a few steps further than they did, to make something meaningful out of their lives.

But my senior year would bring pivotal changes for both of us. We reached a fork in the road, and the decisions we both made during that time would impact my life in ways neither of us could have imagined.

Ten

When it came to choosing the kind of man I wanted to fall in love with, I had no idea what to look for. In fairy tales, the women always had their Prince Charming—someone to ride in on a white horse, rescue them from distress, and slay dragons or conquer foes along the way.

The descriptions were the same: he was tall, dark and handsome, strong and fearless. He was a protector and a provider. Even my favorite romance novels were filled with the heroic stranger who would do everything in his power to protect and take care of the maiden of his desires.

Interestingly, the stories never ventured beyond the rescue after the hero got the girl; what kind of personality did he have? Did he help around the house? Wash dishes? Did he cook? Did he do laundry? Did he believe in a woman's equality beyond serving his needs?

When I was growing up, little girls were raised with the fairy tale notion of being damsels in distress. We were taught, in subtle and not-so-subtle ways, to wait patiently for our knight in shining armor to rescue us. Even with the rise of the feminist movement, this idea lingered—and to some extent, it still does.

Fortunately, today's worldview is different. More women are claiming their independence, building their own lives, and rewriting those outdated narratives. The reasons for this shift may be up for debate, but one thing is certain: it's a change women needed.

This evolution is vital because when girls aren't taught strength and independence early on, they often grow into women who unconsciously wait to be saved. They look for a man to mend their hearts, fix their lives, or give them permission to dream bigger. The waiting is rarely deliberate— most of the time, we don't even realize we're doing it.

That is, until we look back at a string of broken relationships, reflect on the wrong partners we allowed into our lives, or face those painful "aha moments" when someone's true colors emerge, leaving us to wonder, "What the hell was I thinking?"

Reflection is key, because without it, we're doomed to repeat the same mistakes. Worse, we might find ourselves trapped in new dramas that feel heavier and more overwhelming than the old ones. Starting over can feel like a mountain to climb, but clinging to familiar chaos is no better. The real dream, of course, is to live a life free from drama altogether.

Sometimes, I wish life came with a manual for parents—a guidebook that said things like, "At seven, teach her this," or "At fifteen, tell her that." With clear instructions, maybe we'd have been better prepared for the challenges of adulthood. Instead, many of us grew up learning as life unfolded, often painfully, before our eyes.

Back in the day, we had television and books to help us dream. We created 'happiness wish lists' based on fictional television and book characters and storylines that promised perfect lives and fairytale endings. Those dreams often revolved around the idea of relationships—finding a partner who would complete us.

There's nothing wrong with seeking the perfect partner. But as women—especially single mothers—we need to recognize the profound impact a man's presence can have when children are involved. His role goes beyond his relationship with us; it extends to the lessons his actions and behavior teach our sons and daughters.

For a daughter, a man's presence shapes her understanding of how she should be treated. He can teach her she is precious, valued, and worthy of respect. For a son, that same man sets an example of how to treat women—with kindness, dignity, and as equals.

On the other hand, a toxic presence can cause far-reaching damage. Children often absorb negative dynamics, internalizing them as normal. A daughter may grow up believing disrespect is acceptable, while a son may mirror the harmful behaviors he observed. Breaking these cycles requires personal reflection that is intentional, growth, and a conscious decision to demand better—for ourselves and for our children.

The good news? We have the power to improve our story—not just for ourselves, but for the generations that come after us. By choosing to reflect on our experiences, learn from them, and demand better from ourselves, we're doing the rescuing we once thought would come from someone else.

Listen, I know how overwhelming loneliness can be. Been there, done that. Especially if you're a single mother. Finding a good partner before the invention of the mainstream internet was like fishing in an ocean - you just never knew how deep to go, or what you'd come up with.

My brother and I watched Mama struggle all of our lives, especially romantically. It was heartbreaking to see her get invested in someone, or worse, fall in love, only to have the relationship end. Like many women, she wanted to find a good man who could love her and be there for her and her children.

When I was nine or ten, the man who was the love of her life was killed in a motorcycle accident. We were devastated because he seemed like he was the answer to her prayers—and ours. Not long after, when she recovered from his death and met another seemingly respectable man, I was ecstatic.

I didn't have many real-life examples of Prince Charming when I was a little girl. This man came close, but even he didn't win the cigar because his stint in our lives was short-lived. Mama talked about him all the time, bragging about how smart and sweet he was. They chatted on the phone for long hours at night, and she would be giddy when he called the next morning.

Their first date felt like something out of a fairy tale—a real Cinderella moment. The whole neighborhood seemed to be in on it, gathering outside to catch a glimpse of Mama as she prepared to step out. Upstairs, I was helping her get ready, watching as she transformed.

She looked stunning in a two-piece soft lavender silk dress suit that flowed elegantly. Normally, she wore curly or afro-styled wigs, but tonight her natural hair was pressed and loosely pinned up, with soft, semi-curly tresses framing her face. She was glowing.

When she finally came outside, the crowd erupted into claps and murmurs of admiration. Her date arrived, stepping out of his car and walking up to the steps with an air of confidence. Mama introduced him to Durelle and me first, then to the neighbors, who were eagerly watching.

He was unlike any man we typically saw around the building. While one or two of the men in the neighborhood worked minor jobs, professional men were a rarity—unless they were truant officers, social workers, or salesmen.

But this man? He was different. He was polished, handsome, like someone straight off the TV screen. He wore a tailored suit, his hair was neatly cut, and his mustache was perfectly trimmed. When he handed Mama a bouquet of flowers, it was like the moment everyone had been waiting for. It wasn't just wonderful—it was magical.

Then it happened—like the clock striking midnight at the ball. Just as they were preparing to leave, the magic shattered. Mama fell forward, hitting the pavement face-first. Her body went rigid, her limbs stiffening in unnatural jerks as an epileptic seizure overtook her.

My heart sank, the fairy-tale moment dissolving into chaos. All the glamour, all the anticipation, evaporated in an instant. But her date—her Prince Charming—didn't hesitate. He rushed to her side, lifting her off the pavement with a steady strength. Without a word, he carried her back inside the house, his demeanor unshaken.

He laid her gently on the couch, taking the cold towel I handed him and pressing it softly to her forehead. His hands were steady, his concern genuine, as he tried to bring her comfort.

Mama slowly recovered, her eyes fluttering open as she came out of the seizure. He stayed by her side until she was coherent again, his calm presence filling the room. Then, with a kind smile and a promise to call and check on her later, he left.

That call never came.

I wonder—if Cinderella's magical dress had turned to rags in front of Prince Charming, would he have still come searching for her the next day? Or would he, like Mama's date, have walked away, unable to reconcile the fantasy with her truth?

Mama was embarrassed, and I felt her pain as if it were my own. This man had seemed so different from anyone she'd ever been with—kind, respectful, thoughtful. For a moment, it felt like maybe she'd finally found her Prince Charming, after dealing with the Ro's of the world. But even he wasn't ready to handle the reality of her epilepsy.

Later, Mama confided in me that his words stayed with her long after he was gone. While he'd been so gentle that night, cooling her forehead with a damp towel and helping her to the couch, his whispered question had devastated: "Why didn't you tell me?"

It wasn't a question asked out of cruelty, but it cut deep nonetheless. In those six words, he had unintentionally reinforced her greatest fear—that the truth about her condition would scare good men away.

She never met another man like him. She still had her share of relationships, but none of them came close. He was her shot at landing Prince Charming, only to have it snatched away because of a disability she couldn't control. The few men who came after him? Let's just say they were no prizes.

In the early 80s, it wasn't uncommon for young mothers to have their boyfriends move in with them. Some did it out of loneliness or fear. Others moved them in for financial support or to help raise their kids. But Mama was different. She was independent and headstrong—if someone was going to live with us, they had to be special.

Because we wanted her to be happy, we were content with anyone who could make her smile. There was one exception, though, and he turned out to be the man who had the biggest impact on all of our lives. I was fifteen, and my brother was eight when they met. They were introduced by a mutual friend while we were living in the projects. I don't know if it was love at first sight, but he spent the night—and never left.

At first, he seemed cool. But over time, something about him didn't sit right with my brother and me. We talked about it often, trying to put our finger on what made us uncomfortable, but we could never quite figure it out.

My brother looked to me for guidance since I was the oldest. I told him we'd just have to wait and see how things turned out. It wasn't just about us or our gut feelings—it was about Mama finally being happy. And that mattered more than anything.

It didn't take long for our concerns about him to be validated. He drank regularly and seemed to thrive on creating stress in our lives. From falsely accusing me of stealing to slyly calling me every name but the child of God, we couldn't wait for the day Mama would kick him to the curb. Mama didn't play when it came to her kids, so we couldn't understand why he lasted as long as he did.

We lived in a 16-story public housing building on 40th and Oakenwald, just a short walk from Chicago's scenic lakefront. Our three-bedroom apartment, with its burnt orange concrete walls, always felt dim. The bright flowery living room set and shiny hard-tiled floors added a touch of light, but it couldn't erase the heavy atmosphere that came with her irritating boyfriend.

After a few months of him living with us, Mama called Durelle and me to the kitchen table for a talk. We sat down with hopeful hearts, convinced she was about to tell us they had broken up. They'd argued the night before—a regular feature of their relationship—and we were ready for the good news.

"We got married today," she revealed without the joy of a new bride.

Her announcement hit us like a weight crashing down on us. We didn't say a word, but our faces betrayed our shock and disbelief. We stared at each other, our anger growing. How could she marry him—of all people? And worse, how could she do it without telling us?

My brother and I had always wanted a father figure in the house. In the 80s, society insisted that families like ours—single mother struggling with kids—were "broken." We were poor, reliant on the government for every form of subsidy, and Mama rarely seemed happy. We thought these hardships came from not having a man in the house, and we craved the illusion of a so-called "whole" family. So, despite our frustrations, we tried to hope for the best with our new stepfather.

Within weeks, their arguments intensified, the kind that reminded me of the fights her parents used to have. But this time, Mama was the aggressor. Their crazy battles became a regular occurrence, and one of the most explosive took place right on the corner of 43rd Street, in full view of everyone.

After that public blow-up, Mama called the house, snapping angrily over the payphone. "Throw his shit out the window!" she barked at me.

I froze, unsure if I'd heard her right. We lived on the thirteenth floor. Surely, she had to be joking.

"Are you serious?" I asked, laughing on the line.

"Put his shit in a bag and throw it out the window! All of it!" she screamed, bass rumbling in her voice.

I don't know what he did to tick her off that day—it didn't take much. Despite loving him, he brought out her worst, and she morphed into a vision of herself I didn't recognize. Their relationship was a lot like her parents'—volatile, unpredictable, and like oil and water, they didn't mix.

As ordered, I stuffed his things into black garbage bags, marched to the window, and sent them flying. One by one, the bags plummeted to the ground, landing with satisfying thuds. I couldn't help but feel a strange sense of glee. This was it, I thought. She was finally done with him.

But my triumph was short-lived. Barely thirty minutes later, the door opened, and there he was—trailing behind her, both of them carrying his tattered bags of clothes. I couldn't believe it. All that drama, and he was still here.

This kind of chaos became our norm. The third time she barked at me to toss his things out, I just ignored her. What was the point? It was clear by then—he'd always find his way back.

When we're in the thick of a situation, it's hard to see how the environment we create affects our children. The way adults handle sensitive or challenging moments in front of kids shapes how those kids respond to similar situations as adults.

It also influences the choices they make later in life. As the old saying goes, "It starts at home." In dysfunctional surroundings, children subconsciously absorb life lessons by watching their parents or caregivers, for better or worse.

Some lessons in life can be straightforward, shaped by conscious choices. You will always make the right moves if you've been properly prepared. But other lessons come from repeating cycles, and those are the hardest to learn. Most of the time, we don't even realize we're stuck in a cycle until we pause to reflect—and only then after certain choices have already been made.

Eleven

Looking back over my life, I realize many of my own decisions mirrored my mother's. Like hers, they were impulsive and often driven by the moment, a reflection of patterns I hadn't yet recognized.

Mama's choices with her husband set off a chain reaction of events she couldn't have predicted. The true impact my stepfather had on my life went far beyond the petty fights he had with her. As their battles escalated, his anger shifted toward me. At first, it was verbal and psychological. He seemed to take pleasure in finding fault with everything I did.

Even when I brought home straight A's and thrived academically, moments I thought would make them proud, he belittled my accomplishments. His words cut deeper than I wanted to admit, turning what should have been my victories into moments of doubt. Over time, the weight of his criticism began to overshadow my achievements, leaving me questioning if anything I did would ever be good enough.

"You think you're smart. You ain't shit. Anybody can get A's from that high school." He'd laugh in my face and snarl, "You ain't neva gonna be shit."

As someone who had struggled with self-esteem issues for most of my life, my stepfather's words hit me like stakes driven straight through my heart. Even though I never saw him as a parental figure, his taunts hurt.

Mama would stand up for me, yelling at him to stop talking to me that way. But in the next breath, she'd excuse his behavior, brushing it off as a symptom of his drinking. "Baby, he's just drunk," she'd say, as if that made it better. "He really loves you like a daughter."

Her words were meant to comfort, but they only added to my confusion. How could love and hurt coexist like that? It was a question that lingered, shaping how I made sense of love and worth for years to come.

The desire to view people through rose-colored lenses is strong, especially when we want something so badly. We'll drum up excuses for why they aren't living up to expectations, not wanting to admit they simply can't.

When someone's heart is deeply invested, their perception of the other person becomes tied to the fantasy of what they wish was true—even if that vision is a lie. I never saw him as a father —not even a drunk one—and I doubt Mama did either. She saw the man she hoped he could be, the father she wanted for us. But he couldn't be that man.

When he crossed the line one night when I was seventeen, I thought she would finally see him for who he really was.

They came home late from a party, their voices already raised in an argument as they stepped into the apartment. I was on the phone with my friend Michelle C., but curiosity—or maybe concern—got the best of me. I hung up, opened my bedroom door, and stepped out.

The moment he spotted me, he zeroed in. "What the hell are you lookin' at? And what stinks in this house? Is it you?" His words were filled with venom, matching the glare in his eyes, followed by that irritating drunken laugh I had come to despise.

I wanted to snap back, "Don't start with me tonight," but I held my tongue out of respect. No matter how much I hated him, I always maintained respect. Instead, I rolled my eyes in silent teenage rebellion, which felt like the only power I had.

That simple gesture pissed him off. He exploded into one of his tirades, spewing more insults to tear me down. But I had reached my limit. I fired back, meeting his verbal assault with my own. I was tired of being told I was worthless, tired of biting my tongue. For once, I let him know exactly how I felt.

Thankfully, my little brother wasn't home. As the argument grew louder, Mama's voice cut through our yelling as she pleaded with us to stop, but neither of us listened. His anger boiled over, and suddenly, he stormed toward me. I barely had time to react before his chest collided with mine, shoving me back a step.

Mama quickly stepped between us, her hands up in desperation as she tried to calm him. "Stop it! Go to bed," she demanded, her voice trembling as she glared at her husband. But he wasn't done. He brushed past her, his chest pressing against me, forcing me back until my shoulder blades hit the wall.

My heart raced as I stared at him with rage. I clenched my fists at my sides, swallowing back the lump of fear rising in my throat. I would not cry—I wouldn't give him that satisfaction —but my anger burned hotter with every second.

"Get off of me!" I yelled, trying to push him away.

He was over six feet tall with a stocky build, so moving him was difficult.

He was so close I could smell the alcohol on his breath. When my mother was able to finally pull him away, she yelled at me to go into my room. As I stomped in that direction, I felt a painful crack to the side of my head, followed quickly by a sharp sting. I didn't know what happened at first, but when I turned around, I saw him standing with a wooden bat in his hand, his face snarled like that of a madman.

My stepfather had bashed me in the ear with a baseball bat.

I lost all sense of reasoning as the months of criticisms and negative taunts overwhelmed me. I used strength from some unknown source to run up on him, knocking him backward onto the floor. Chaos ensued as I pummeled him, screaming like a mad person, while my ear pulsated in pain.

My mother pulled me up finally, and while holding him in place, she pleaded for me to go to my room.

As I stumbled in that direction, another sharp blow landed, this time to the back of my head. A searing pain shot through my skull as I swayed forward, my hand instinctively flying to the spot. Warm blood trickled between my fingers, and the world spun around me. My knees threatened to buckle, and for a terrifying moment, I thought I was going to pass out.

But then, piercing through my haze, I heard Mama scream from another room. Her cry jolted me back to reality like a lightning strike. The dizziness faded into raw adrenaline as panic surged through me. I ran straight for the phone, my trembling fingers fumbling over the buttons as I dialed 911.

"He's going crazy!" I screamed into the receiver when the operator asked what was the emergency, my voice shaking with fear and desperation. "My stepfather's attacking us!"

The operator who instructed me to be quiet and let her listen while she was dispatching officers to the house could hear Mama's screams in the background. She heard my stepfather yell, "Bitch, I'll kill you! I'll kill every last one of y'all in here!" When I stepped into the kitchen, still holding the phone, they were against the sink, wrestling over an air rifle after he bashed it on Mama's wrist.

Within minutes, the police were banging on the door, and I ran to open it. My stepfather was arrested on the spot. The paramedics looked after my mother and started patching me up, telling mama we both needed to be taken to the emergency room.

As we were being escorted to the ambulance, I saw the police paddy wagon rocking, and I smiled as I imagined the officers, all Black men, beating the hell out of my stepfather for the assault he brought on us. It would later be confirmed. That is exactly what happened.

While receiving painful stitches on the inside of my ear and the back of my head at the hospital, I was sure his presence in our lives was over. After all, he had done the unthinkable; he put his hands on Izora's child. What kind of grown man would hit a teenage girl with a bat? While her wrist was being bandaged, she promised he would be gone forever.

When we got home early that next morning, the air felt different—heavier somehow. It was as if the walls themselves were still holding onto the tension. Everything seemed surreal as I took in the fight's aftermath. The living room was a mess, with overturned furniture and fragments of the chaos scattered all over.

Mama and I sat at the kitchen table, the same place where she had once announced her marriage to him. Now, it became the setting for a very different conversation. Her face was stained with regret as she apologized to me for bringing him into our lives. Then her tone darkened.

"I think he wanted you, Mimi," she said quietly.

Hearing those words from my mother was like a punch to the gut. For her to admit such a thing—about her own husband, no less—must have been devastating. How long had she carried that fear? How long had she suspected? My mind immediately jumped to something that had happened just a few months earlier. Because she had been brave enough to share her fears, I was encouraged to tell her what I had kept to myself.

One weekend I was in my room doing what I always did— lying on my bed listening to music. I was so engrossed in the eighty's cuts playing from my homemade cassette that I didn't hear the door open. When I felt a presence, I looked up.

He was standing in the doorway, glaring at me. He didn't say a word—he just stared. I did not know how long he'd been there, and after a few awkward seconds, he closed the door. I shrugged it off as him just being weird, but her declaration brought new meaning to that moment.

However, two days after her apology and confession, Mama's love for him and her unyielding belief that he was redeemable made it as if that conversation or the events that landed us both in the emergency room never took place. She called me to her room and passed the telephone to me.

"Who is it?" I asked, expecting it to be my best friend.

"It's your stepdaddy."

I was dumbfounded, and my upbeat mood changed fiercely. "Mama, I have nothing to say to him," I hissed, handing the phone back. I looked at her questioningly, wondering why she was even speaking to him.

"Just talk to him, Mimi," she pleaded. "He's really sorry. Just talk to him."

I didn't understand the rationale behind what she was asking me to do. For her, and only for her, I begrudgingly took the phone. The man was a monster to me after what he did. I didn't just hate him; I also feared him. I half listened as he begged for absolution, proclaiming how sorry he was and how he never meant to hurt me. He made promises to get himself together and repeated the lie he told my mother—that he loved me like a daughter.

His words fell on deaf ears, and I quickly passed the phone back to my mother. I stomped out of her room, pissed that the two days of peace we quickly became accustomed to in his absence were suddenly gone.

When I heard her complete the call with him, I went back to her room. "Mama, please tell me you're not going to let him come back here."

"Nah, baby. He's not coming back."

I breathed a sigh of relief as her words set me at ease. She had never lied to me, and I had no reason to believe she wasn't being truthful. I saw her walk away from any man who even looked like he would bring harm to her children. The assault notwithstanding, because I'd finally let my guard down and told her about her husband's inappropriate behavior, I was confident she wouldn't let him back into our lives.

I started to doubt everything when his daily collect calls to the house kept getting accepted. The day before we were supposed to go to court, he begged for my forgiveness again. But what really shook me was my mother backing him up, trying to convince me he'd changed into some loving father figure. I couldn't wrap my head around it. What was happening to her? Why couldn't she see through him? What kind of hold did he have on her?

I went to court the next day with my mind made up; I was pressing charges against the man who had brutally assaulted me and my mother, and who threatened to kiss us all. She couldn't see him, but I did. As officers escorted him into the courtroom in handcuffs, the scowl on his face when he looked at me reinforced just how much he hated me.

His desperate pleas for forgiveness and his loud proclamations of regret over the phone weren't about remorse—they were calculated moves to manipulate my mother into shielding him from the punishment he knew he deserved. The fear he used to instill in me crumbled as I realized something I'd never considered before: I held the power to send him away, to protect myself, and to ensure he wouldn't hurt me—or my mother—again.

The judge asked if we were prepared to press charges. My mother and I answered in stark contradiction. "Yes, your honor," I said boldly, while she replied, "No, your honor."

I was stunned. I didn't understand the power he had over her heart. It seemed to be so strong that the desire to save her love appeared to overwhelm the protective factor of her daughter.

Sensing the tension between us, the judge called for a fifteen-minute recess, giving me and my mother time to talk things over. In my mind, though, there was nothing to discuss. I knew exactly what I wanted—I wanted him to go to jail.

When we stepped outside the courtroom and into the cold hallway, my mother sat next to me on a bench and quietly begged me to reconsider. "Mimi, don't do this. This is my life you're taking away!"

I couldn't believe my ears. I was hurt and confused, and I saw her as one of those women who put their men above their children. My respect for her was shattered in that moment and I didn't realize how damaged our relationship would become after that. One thing was certain: I could no longer be around that man.

"I'll drop the charges on one condition," I bargained. "You have to let me live with Auntie, because I can't live there with him."

I was seventeen, still in high school, and didn't have a job. Yet, I was in a position of negotiating a major turning point in my life. I didn't care about the consequences of my demands. I didn't imagine there could be any. She wanted her husband free, and I wanted to be free of his presence. We agreed I would move in with my aunt. When we were called back into the courtroom, I told the judge that I changed my mind and was dropping the charges.

The judge looked me square in the eyes and asked, "Were you coerced in any way to change your decision?"

I said no, but I knew she wasn't convinced. However, there was no more she could do. She ordered my stepfather to be released.

Mama and I left the courthouse, the tension between us higher than ever. On the bus ride home, the only solace I had was knowing I would be moving out as he settled back in. We stopped at One Stop, the neighborhood grocery store, to pick up a bag of frozen catfish steaks and a forty-ounce bottle of Old English beer—his favorite food and drink.

She wanted to prepare a celebratory dinner for his return. For reasons I couldn't fully understand, she truly loved that man, and he made her happy, even if he brought chaos into our lives.

He arrived at the apartment less than an hour later and immediately started an argument with my mother. When she tried to calm him down, he snapped. "Fuck you and these triflin' ass kids of yours! I don't need you motherfuckers!" His tone was sharper, more violent than ever.

I was on the phone with my aunt, making plans to move in, when she overheard them arguing in the background.

"Get the hell out of there—now," she demanded.

I tried to protest, hesitant to leave, but she was adamant. "Take your brother and go. Don't argue with me."

Reluctantly, my brother and I left, their shouting voices trailing behind us as we walked down the ramp to the elevator. He hadn't witnessed the first attack, and I was determined to keep him from seeing whatever might happen next.

As we stood at the bus stop, tense and frightened, we kept looking back to the window of our apartment, as if we expected to see some movement that would tell us what was going on inside. Anger mixed with worry churned in my chest. I was furious that Mama had let him back into our lives. I was afraid of what he might do to her.

But amidst all the fear and frustration, one thought brought me a sliver of relief: I wouldn't have to live with his madness anymore.

Or so I thought.

I left on Friday. By Sunday morning, Mama had ordered me to come back home. My stepfather had again somehow convinced her he was a changed man, despite blowing up the moment he walked through the door after being released from jail and threatening to kill us all.

I reminded her of the promise she made and the conversation we'd had about her concerns over his intentions toward me. But she wouldn't listen. Her resolve seemed to vanish, replaced by blind faith in his empty words. "Everything will be okay," she assured me.

Only the individual knows why he or she makes the decisions they do, even if it appears crazy to other people. Having children can exacerbate problems caused by those decisions, because the wrong choices can damage the entire family.

Mama loved her husband, and she loved her kids. She wanted her family to work and believed it could, even if she had to mold it with her own tears and pain. I later learned from my own experiences the depths to which we as women sometimes allow our emotions to take us when we are in love.

She still held on to the idea that this man would turn into the Prince Charming she thought she needed, and we all would live happily ever after. Without realizing it, my mother was suffering through emotional and psychological abuse, and it was being cycled down to her children, particularly to me.

Twelve

M y boyfriend at the time—I'll call him Kwame—was exactly the kind of person I always seemed drawn to: an outcast, someone whose underlying issues mirrored my own. Although he didn't live in subsidized housing like I did, his home life and upbringing were just as chaotic. We first met when I was 13 and he was 15, but it wasn't until I was 16, during a chance meeting at a mutual friend's house, that we reconnected and started dating.

In his own way, he was my knight in shining armor. He was eighteen, a high school dropout, and struggled to keep a steady job. Yet, he always made me feel special. He'd buy me little presents and travel from the north side of the city to the south side to see me every single day, even if it meant walking the entire way. He didn't have much, but his dedication and loyalty hooked me.

My stepfather didn't like him, and that heavily influenced how my mother felt about him. But he was there for me when everything in my house fell apart. I saw him as my strength, my greatest ally. When Mama lost all credibility with me—after trying to convince me to forgive the man who had assaulted both of us—he stepped into the void she left behind.

He became my best friend, the one I leaned on. Even though her concerns about him would later prove to be valid, I ignored anything negative she had to say. To me, he wasn't just a boyfriend; he was my refuge in the middle of all the dysfunction.

Returning to the madness that had become the norm in Mama's house only confirmed that nothing had changed. My stepfather moved through the apartment with a permanent scowl, directing his malice at me as if I had committed some unforgivable crime. His disdain deepened whenever my boyfriend came over, and the tension in the house felt like a powder keg waiting to explode. I feared that when it did, the consequences would be even worse than before.

And then, I found out I was pregnant.

I was bright, full of potential, and college-bound. Through Mama's experiences, I had seen what having a child at a young age could mean for my life. Yet, despite knowing better, I was on the verge of repeating her cycles, unable—or perhaps unwilling—to connect the dots between her choices and my own. Blaming my environment would have been easy.

But the truth was more complicated. I wasn't a little girl anymore. I was an intelligent 17-year-old. I should have protected myself, but emotionally, I clung to neediness, like a child holding onto a tattered security blanket. Even as I moved into young adulthood, I carried the belief that I needed to be rescued, which led me into shallow relationships with men who were as broken as I was. The would-be father of my children was no exception.

He was a mirror of me in so many ways—a reflection of my trauma and unresolved pain. Having endured his own childhood abuse, he latched onto me in search of the same superficial love and validation I craved. His needs quickly became bigger than mine, but I couldn't see it. Like Mama with my stepfather, I was blinded by the fairytale I had written in my heart. I believed I could fix him, that together we could heal each other.

Getting pregnant didn't soften the tension in the house; it made things worse. My stepfather seized every opportunity to berate me, reveling in his chance to prove me a failure. "I told you!" he sneered. "I knew you weren't gonna be shit! I hate you! I'll kill you, that nigga, and that baby!"

Mama tried in vain to understand the root of his unwarranted hatred for me. When he demanded that my boyfriend stay away from the house, she gave in. She still saw his dislike for Kwame as paternal protectiveness, not the irrational jealousy it really was.

I was floored when she came into my room and announced her decision to side with her husband. Whether it was pregnancy hormones or sheer exhaustion from dealing with my stepfather's madness, I snapped at her—something I had never done before.

"Mama, this makes no sense. I'm pregnant!" I cried, frustration and emotion boiling over. "At least he's coming around and not running away like most guys do when they get a girl pregnant. You're just doing this to please your crazy husband!"

Her shock was immediate, and she reacted instinctively, shoving me against the wall. "You heard what I said!" she shouted.

For the first and only time in my life, I pushed her back, the fear and respect I had always held for her evaporating. At that moment, I knew it was time to leave her house for good. Reluctantly, my mother agreed.

I made arrangements to move in with my paternal great-grandmother. It wasn't ideal, but it was safer than staying in a home where I was constantly threatened by my stepfather. That night, I packed up the few belongings I had, determined to walk out and never look back.

But he wasn't about to let me leave in peace. As I approached the door, he stepped in front of me, blocking my way with a glare full of rage. My heart pounded so hard I thought it might break free from my chest. Then he pressed into me with force, his body shoving mine until I stumbled back. For a moment, I froze, fear washing over me as memories of his past violence flooded my mind.

But I wouldn't let him win. Summoning every ounce of courage I had, I sidestepped him and walked out, leaving him —and his madness—behind.

His hatred and the fear he instilled in me would haunt me for years. As I left my childhood home that night—seventeen years young and pregnant—I stepped into adulthood woefully unprepared for what lay ahead. The cycle was in full effect, and I was carrying it with me into the next chapter of my life.

Thirteen

I made the decision to leave my mother's house for several reasons, but the main one was concern for my health and safety. Still, I did not know the whirlwind I was stepping into when I took that leap. Looking back, I often wonder: would I make the same choice knowing what I know now?

Maybe I could have roughed it out, found a way to endure the psychological abuse from my stepfather. But the fear of his ability to hurt me—physically and emotionally—was too great. He had already proven he was capable, and I lost faith that my mother could protect me from him. Her perspective on his ability to be a father figure was different from mine, and I couldn't reconcile that.

From being molested, bullied, and teased, to enduring my stepfather's cruelty, I stumbled into adulthood on a long, hard road, moving forward in a daze. I didn't enjoy life; I simply existed, blind to the necessity of confronting the trauma I had endured. That revelation wouldn't come until I was well into my thirties.

As the years passed, I saw my mother go through her own transformation. She blossomed into a mature woman who removed the dysfunction of toxic relationships from her life, starting with her husband. She moved mountains for me, helping me secure my own housing and even using her connections to get me my first salaried job at the housing authority.

She became a source of strength and compassion not only for us but for the families in our public housing community, for whom she became a tireless advocate.

We never talked about the past—about my childhood or what happened with her husband—but it lingered in my heart for years, festering into a hidden resentment. There were times I couldn't stand to be around her because I couldn't let go of the feeling that she had chosen her husband over me.

The resentment deepened when I thought about her rejection of my cry for help during one of the darkest moments of my life. When I reached out to her, desperate for refuge from the emotionally and psychologically abusive relationship with the father of my children, she sent me back into the hell I was living.

I didn't understand then that she was trying to teach me something—how to face my mistakes as a woman and take ownership of my decisions. I was too immature to see it, and my anger at her lasted for years. But, like so many of my choices, that anger was misguided. I didn't yet understand what it truly took to be a mother—or a woman.

I only saw what I thought was in front of me: a mother who couldn't protect her children. But now I know there was more to it. She did the best she could with what she knew, and that realization softened the sharp edges of our past.

When a girl's youth is cut short and she is thrust into adulthood before she is ready to handle grown-up responsibilities, the chances for missing out on fundamental lessons needed to guide her through life are high. This happened to my maternal grandmother. It's what happened to my mother. And eventually, it happened to me.

Realizing these patterns drives me to pass on what I've learned to my children as I see them grapple with their life struggles. I carry my own bag of advice, ready to share it with them and any young person I come across who might need guidance.

When faced with decisions like those I had to make at a young age—such as leaving home—it's critical to weigh every factor. My situation was delicate, even dangerous at times. But moving out on my own and stepping into the real world was terrifying.

When I meet young people considering the same path, I ask them: Is it safe where you are? Is it a healthy environment? Take a hard, realistic look at your situation. Because treading into the unknown, without preparation, can be far more dangerous to your mental and emotional well-being than you realize.

I often wrestled with the judgments I made, knowing how deeply they shaped my life. Life taught me it's impossible to predict the outcome of every situation or to always have the clarity to weigh every decision and its consequences. But what we can do is approach choices with as much wisdom and thoughtfulness as possible.

Leaving home at the tender age of seventeen was daunting. In my mind, it was necessary—but that didn't make it easy. Add the fact that I was pregnant, and the result was a tangled, emotional soul with no logical sense of direction. I was unprepared for the harsh realities of the world, just as my mother had been when she took that same leap.

We both learned the hard way.

Dealing with my stepfather was tough; being on my own was tougher. I had a baby growing inside of me, and I missed my mother and little brother. At the same time, I was still holding on to anger and resentment. That mixture of emotions put me in a dark funk as I saw my life spinning out of control. Many nights I cried while staring up at the stars from the window in the tiny bedroom of my great-grandmother's house, searching for answers that would never come.

I wished for my daddy––not Ro, the man I knew as a child, but my deceased biological father. Emotionally, I was still a little girl struggling with grown-up decisions and situations. It was painfully obvious I wasn't ready.

Kwame was out on the street "hustling," as he called it, trying to get money so we could find a place to live together. My great-grandmother was old school and wouldn't allow us to live under the same roof. In fact, he had to leave after ten in the evening and could never stay overnight.

He couldn't get a steady job because he had a criminal record. So, he did odd jobs and stood on the street begging for money. I would later learn there was more to this hustle, making my decisions even more perilous. Eventually, he befriended someone who took pity on our situation and allowed us to use his spare bedroom.

The benefactor was a white college professor who lived alone on the north side of the city and met Kwame while he was soliciting for money on the subway. The professor saw us as a young family trying to get a fresh start on life and opened his doors to us. Having been informed about my history with my stepfather, he tried everything in his power to make me feel comfortable.

"You make yourself at home," he told me, with a slight Georgia drawl. "I want you to feel like this is your place, you hear me?"

He was such a sweetheart. I tried to do as he said, but I couldn't. Things felt foreign. Eventually, I realized I was trading one form of stress for another. During our stay with him, I realized the father of my unborn child was addicted to crack cocaine.

Crack was a devastating thorn in the Black community during the 1980s, leaving no one untouched. It was so pervasive that almost everyone either knew someone or was related to someone who struggled with addiction. The epidemic swept through urban neighborhoods with alarming speed, its destruction indescribable.

It didn't take a psychologist to understand the devastating effects of addiction. It destroyed the mind, crushed the spirit, and stripped away the decency of those who fell under its grip. Addiction made people do things they'd never imagine themselves capable of, and crack unleashed the absolute worst demons within. The father of my children became a living, breathing testament to the ruin this drug could cause.

The first time I saw him use was at a party in 1987, a few months after I learned I was pregnant. He reassured me it was nothing serious, just another way to get high—no stronger than marijuana, he claimed. I believed him. How could I not? I didn't drink, didn't smoke, and had no experience with drugs. I was completely naïve.

He pulled out a small glass pipe with a bulb at the end and placed a white, chalky piece inside. Flicking a lighter beneath the bulb, he heated the rock until it began to melt, filling the pipe with smoke. He brought it to his lips and inhaled deeply. The sound of it—sharp and crackling—sent a chill through me.

I couldn't put my finger on why, but something about the whole scene unnerved me. It was the way the lighter's flame danced under the glass, the way his focus shifted as he exhaled, the intensity of it all. It felt wrong—dangerous. And even though I didn't fully understand why, I couldn't shake the sinking feeling that I was witnessing something far worse than he had let on.

After we moved in together, I understood that fear. It mocked me for making grown-up decisions that put me in situations my young mind was not prepared to handle––things such as living in a stranger's apartment with my drug-addicted boyfriend, along with being pregnant and on the verge of dropping out of high school.

We lived with the professor for only a few months, but it felt like a lifetime. I was confronted with some realities about life that stunted any of the joy I thought I would experience being on my own. When I think back on that time, I almost feel removed from it. Pain, anger, and remorse intertwined into one solid coil of depression, sucking the little scrap of happiness from me.

The professor was the one who broke the news to me about Kwame's addiction. It all unraveled on a wild, chaotic night, a whirlwind of revelations that exposed the truth about his and my boyfriend's relationship. In a single evening, my new, semi-independent world was flipped completely upside down.

The events unfolded with my mother's frustration reaching a boiling point. She was fed up with me missing school and tried to force me back home by sending the police to the professor's house.

When the officers arrived, I explained my situation, and they informed her that, at seventeen—and just two weeks shy of turning eighteen—they couldn't legally make me leave. I felt a strange sense of triumph, a small victory in asserting my independence. To celebrate, the professor gave Kwame some money, which I assumed was meant to host a small party.

Five hours later, with no sign of Kwame, the professor, now visibly drunk and seething with anger, dropped a bombshell that knocked me on my ass. He revealed Kwame was supposed to use most of the money he'd been given to find a young man for the professor to sleep with—an arrangement that had apparently been going on since we moved in. Because the professor was keeping his sexuality hidden for fear of losing his job, this was kept from me.

And then, to top it off, he told me Kwame was addicted to crack cocaine and had stolen the money. Not only was the father of my unborn child acting as a quasi-pimp, but he was also battling an addiction that I hadn't even realized was there. Every word hit me like a wrecking ball, demolishing any illusion of stability I had left.

This professor, who had always seemed so kind and generous, revealed a side of himself I never expected. Through drunken tears, he angrily threatened that if Kwame didn't "bring his Black ass back" with either the money or the man he'd promised, we'd both be out on the street. His words, slurred and sharp, shattered the image I had of him and left me reeling.

I was so shaken, I left the house in the middle of the night, braving a snowstorm on Chicago's north side. Guided only by fragments of memory, I wandered the streets, determined to find Kwame. The biting cold of Chicago's infamous "hawk" tore through me as I searched for over an hour, finally stumbling upon the building where he had first shown me his drug use. Just as I feared, there he was—getting high.

When he saw me, his face went from shock to anger in seconds. But his fury wasn't directed at me; it was aimed squarely at the professor.

The next day, after sobering up, the professor was filled with remorse. He was disgusted with how he had treated me and spent the following weeks trying everything he could to make amends. But the damage was done. My trust in him had been shattered, and even more so, my faith in Kwame was irreparably broken. He had shown me, in no uncertain terms, that he couldn't be relied upon—not as a partner, and not as the father of our unborn child.

With nowhere else to go, I felt trapped—forced to choose between staying in this toxic situation or returning home to my mother and stepfather. Going back wasn't an option, so I stayed with Kwame.

Nights on that tiny, enclosed porch-turned-bedroom were long and lonely. I would lie awake, wondering where he was or what had happened to him. Sometimes, I feared he had finally abandoned me and our unborn baby. Other times, I worried he had crossed the wrong person and paid the ultimate price for his choices.

Eventually, he would stumble back after days of being on a crack binge, his absence explained but never justified. Each time he left, my hope dwindled a little more, and each time he returned, my resolve was tested again.

The professor checked into rehab for alcoholism, which meant we had to leave. With nowhere else to turn, we moved in with Kwame's mother and stepfather—a decision that plunged me into an even more chaotic environment. Both were heavy drinkers, and their constant arguments echoed through the house at all hours, creating a tense and volatile atmosphere.

If that wasn't bad enough, the house was infested with rats— enormous ones, as big as my foot. At night, when the lights went out, I'd lie awake, my ears attuned to the sound of them squeaking and scurrying across the floor. The worst part was feeling them move inside the couch where we slept, their small bodies shifting beneath me like a living nightmare. Each squeak and shuffle sent shivers through my spine, turning sleep into an impossibility.

A few months after my first daughter was born, a small beacon of hope appeared: my mother helped me secure a Section 8 voucher for subsidized housing. With it, I was finally able to get an apartment of my own—a step toward independence that felt like a huge victory.

We were so eager to move that there was no time (or money) for fancy packing. Instead, we stuffed everything we owned into oversized plastic garbage bags, balancing everything awkwardly as we hoisted them and our baby onto the L—the iconic Chicago train system. Destination: the Southside neighborhood of West Englewood. It wasn't perfect, but it was ours, and for the first time, it felt like a fresh start.

For those of us without cars, the L was indispensable—a symbol of movement and possibility, even when weighed down by the baggage of life, literally and figuratively. As the train rattled and screeched its way along the tracks, the weight of those garbage bags mirrored the emotional weight I carried. But the promise of a new beginning, however tenuous, gave me a taste of optimism. West Englewood was no paradise, but it was my new home, and that felt like a step in the right direction.

My first place, a one-bedroom garden apartment on south Marshfield Avenue, was small but cozy, a space I could have been proud of. Yet, the bubble of despair that seemed to follow me everywhere overshadowed the joy I thought I would feel. Instead of stressing out in someone else's chaotic space, I now had my own home—a quiet place to face my misery alone. Kwame became more unreliable, his disappearing acts and drug use spiraling out of control.

I was only eighteen, navigating a world I wasn't equipped to handle. Though I was living in grown-up situations and shouldering grown-up responsibilities, my mind couldn't keep up with the turmoil surrounding me. I was like an ant, trying to find my way through the giant muddled mess I was in. The world felt massive, overwhelming—a maze I was too small to navigate.

The cycle was in full effect.

As Kwame's addiction spiraled, my goals began slipping further out of reach. Instead of focusing on my future, I became consumed by him and his problems. I had promised myself—and my mother—that I would not fail in school and would take summer classes to earn my high school diploma.

When we were staying with the professor months earlier, pregnancy made getting to school every day an uphill battle. Morning sickness was hard enough, but braving Chicago's brutal winter and commuting on the L left me physically drained and emotionally depleted.

Eventually, it all became too overwhelming, and I dropped out —just six months shy of graduating. Letting go of the academic success I had worked so hard to achieve was heartbreaking, so I vowed to attend summer school and finish. Yet, despite my best intentions, I broke that promise.

Nights continued to be stressful and lonely. Days were hard as I struggled to figure out a way to turn the tide in my life. To make matters worse, by the time I was twenty, my third child was on the way. It made no logical sense to have more than one kid with an unemployed crack head who had a criminal rap sheet dating back to when he was thirteen.

But there was no thinking at the time; there was only existing as I woke up in the mornings and stared at life being played out on Oprah and the soap operas. I went to bed at night, having accomplished nothing productive that could move my young family and myself forward.

I seldom ventured outside except to go to the store or travel to the laundromat. I didn't visit with my best friend. I was still angry with Mama, so I didn't visit her, and I didn't communicate with family members. The kids and their father were my existence.

Although I loved my children beyond words, I was depressed by the constant strain of watching the man I loved turn into a walking zombie. I was exhausted as I defended my home from the onslaught of trouble he brought regularly because of his drug abuse. Going outside—even if only to get fresh air— seemed pointless.

One afternoon, while trying to find another apartment that would take my Section 8, I saw a rainbow. The multicolored arc filled me with such an emotional jolt, and I couldn't contain the joy and hope that flooded my heart, spilling out through my tears as I walked down the street. I'd heard about rainbows, saw them in books and movies, but it was the first time I saw one up close.

When you feel dejected, sometimes the smallest things can bring joy into your life and remind you there is a greater purpose.

With all the sadness and despair going on, that surreal vision solidified my connection with God and renewed my faith that everything, in its time, would be all right. I needed that assurance more than ever because it felt like the world was on my shoulders.

As a child, I didn't fathom the difficulties of raising children and taking care of a home. I ventured into that stage financially, emotionally, and mentally unprepared. Adulting was not what I envisioned it to be. I used to see bills come in the mail when I was a kid, but I didn't make the connection between those bills and the lights and gas being on.

When I became an adult, the bills started coming in my name, and suddenly, I was responsible for paying them. I learned quickly that bill collectors don't care about your circumstances—they just want their money. Whether you have no job or a house full of small children, your sob stories mean nothing to them. As a result, we endured many dark, cold nights when the gas and electricity were shut off.

It was difficult to make the adjustment of being the sole provider for my family. Kwame and I had the grandiose idea in the beginning that we would both get jobs and be able to take care of each other and our kids, despite the reality of his circumstances and of me dropping out of high school.

Welfare was my only source of income. With it, I paid what bills I could manage, bought food, and, more often than I'd like to admit, supported my man's drug habit. His hunger for getting high far exceeded the little money I had. When those funds ran out, he started taking things from the house to sell on the streets.

I was slowly becoming the kind of woman I had seen growing up—waiting each month for the fleeting happiness that came with a public aid check and food stamps. Thankfully, my rent was subsidized, and my new landlord often overlooked the fifty dollars I was supposed to pay to supplement the Section 8 assistance.

But the old man's leniency wasn't out of kindness; he had nefarious reasons. As the old saying goes, 'he saw me coming' the moment he interviewed me for the apartment on East 51st Street. He asked probing questions about me, my children, and their father. Based on my age and the fact that I had no job, he pieced together a judgment of me shaped by stereotypes.

On several occasions, he knocked on my door when he knew I was alone. Aware of my boyfriend's addiction, he would offer advice while attempting to capitalize on what he perceived as the stupidity of a young, helpless woman. At first, he hinted at what he wanted. When I played dumb, his advances became more obvious as he suggested his willingness to help me out, but only if I helped him out sexually.

Vulnerability can be misconstrued as desperation in a troubled young woman. If she's not careful, she can open herself up to being used and even abused by those who prey on naïve souls and hearts.

Not only was he old enough to be my grandfather, but he was also married and had children who were twice my age. He soon learned I wasn't the kind of girl whom he could bed with the promise of "putting some change" in my pockets.

Once, when my portion of the rent was behind by several months, he intensified his pressure with threats of evicting me, all the while slithering up to me like a snake in an oil pit as he put his hand under my shirt. I felt sick as his wrinkled, spongy hand grabbed my breast, squeezing while his dull brown eyes gazed into mine, hoping to see a glimmer of interest.

I thought about women who had to endure worse to make ends meet. I also thought about the struggles Mama must have gone through in the early days as she tried to take care of me on her own with no job and no other income except that which was provided by the state.

As I removed his hand from under my blouse, I told him to do what he had to do, even if that meant putting us in the street. I would not give him my body at any cost. I may have been young and struggling like hell, but I was not willing to part my legs with an old man for a few dollars.

Eventually, he gave up on me and did not renew my lease. He had good reason, my turning down his advances notwithstanding. Kwame had kicked in the apartment door so many times, usually after I locked him out to keep him from selling our food and furniture for crack, that I had to prop it closed with a two-by-four.

The landlord hated him for destroying his property. Over time, my situation became more trouble than it was worth in his eyes, especially after I refused to sleep with him.

I can imagine how he must have thought of me. He and society in general saw me as another young welfare queen who had thrown her life away with a deadbeat man. That's not who I was. However, the poor decisions I made reenforced those images to people who didn't know what I was living with and, subsequently, surviving through.

I reference surviving because that's exactly what I was doing. The things I witnessed and experienced while living with a drug addict could have been enough to send me over the edge and into that lost world right along with him. Without realizing it at the time, I was going through similar experiences as my mother when she was with Ro and living out her worst nightmare.

The crack epidemic of the eighties was not just something that was portrayed in New Jack City. It was real. I saw husbands pimp their wives, and parents use their kids as pawns to solicit money from unsuspecting caring strangers so they could score drugs.

I'll never forget the homeless married couple that moved in with us shortly after meeting Kwame at a crack house. Both husband and wife were addicted to the drug, had a small child, and the wife was pregnant. They weren't dirty and disheveled like most street addicts I saw. The husband looked like he had been a professional man, and his wife looked like she had once been a beautiful woman.

The husband bragged about his former years as an executive and how much money he used to make. He touted the lavish lifestyle he once afforded his wife, all while inhaling poison smoke from a crack pipe.

During the day, he would take his wife and their young child to downtown Chicago or Hyde Park, where they begged for money. She was the one stationed out front, cradling the baby in her arms, her dirty and weary face drawing the pity of the unsuspecting public. Meanwhile, he lingered in the background, out of sight, knowing the sympathy factor worked more in her favor.

Afterward, they would return to our apartment, their pockets lined with cash, ready to get high with Kwame. The baby, innocent and oblivious, would lie quietly nearby as the room filled with the acrid smell of crack smoke. It was a heartbreaking routine, one that left a bitter taste in my mouth every time I watched it unfold.

The husband would only allow his wife to have a couple of hits from the pipe, using her pregnancy as an excuse to deny her more. She would scream and cry because, as she said, she worked for it. Her pregnancy didn't stop him from beating her, and after he punched her in the stomach, I demanded he leave my house. I offered to let the wife and baby remain with us.

Like so many abused women, she wouldn't stay unless he was with her. I tried reasoning with her, woman to woman, offering what little wisdom I was only beginning to understand myself. But my words fell on deaf ears, and in the end, I had to make the hard decision to put them all out.

Kwame wasn't happy, but he understood. They were his in-house suppliers, bringing in more drugs than he could ever hustle up on his own. Still, even he had a line—and beating a pregnant woman crossed it.

I thank God I never fell into drug use myself. Being an enabler was hard enough—I endured the impact of addiction on an emotional, psychological, and financial level. Kwame had an escape, however temporary, as the drugs dulled his senses and numbed any shame he might have felt for the things he did to get high. I, on the other hand, had no such escape. I faced every raw emotion, every painful ordeal, with nothing to soften the blow of his addiction's consequences.

Whenever the money ran out—which never took long—he turned to selling whatever little we had left. Televisions, clothes, furniture—most of it donated—nothing in our home was safe. Eventually, even the food disappeared. But the moment that broke me was when he sold the baby's diapers and cans of formula. That was when I realized he was completely lost, and he was dragging us down with him.

I spent four long years trying to reach the vibrant, strong-willed man I had fallen in love with. I fought to save him from the addiction that consumed him, pouring so much of myself into the effort that I barely recognized who I'd become. Night after night, I cried, desperate to understand what I had done to bring such heartbreak and chaos into my life.

The cause was there all along, but when you're deep in the trenches, it's almost impossible to see. Everyone else can see it but when you're inside the bubble, reality feels distorted—like you're looking at the world through a foggy, cracked lens.

I learned to adapt quickly, especially after too many nights of going hungry while waiting for food stamps to come through. Each time I went grocery shopping, I'd open packages and divide the food into Ziploc™ bags, then hide them in places Kwame wouldn't think to look. The baby's formula became my top priority—I stashed cans in different spots around the house, treating them like precious gold.

Even with money, I had to get creative. A few dollars here and there would go into unlikely hiding places, like inside the intercom system. These little survival tactics weren't just about making ends meet; they were about protecting what little we had from being swallowed up by his addiction.

Why did I allow myself to go through this dysfunction instead of just leaving him?

I never had a good enough answer. Other than the obvious one. It's heartbreaking to realize how many women stay in abusive relationships, even when the abuse isn't physical. Studies show that nearly 1 in 4 women in the United States will experience some form of intimate partner violence in their lifetime. While physical abuse tends to grab headlines, emotional and psychological abuse—manipulation, gaslighting, control—often goes unseen and unreported.

According to the National Domestic Violence Hotline, 48% of women in abusive relationships report being emotionally abused, and many stay because of fear, financial dependency, or a belief that things might change.

The heartbreaking truth is that non-physical abuse can be just as damaging, leaving scars that take years to heal. Many of us stay because we think, "Well, at least he doesn't hit me," not realizing that the absence of bruises doesn't mean the absence of harm.

I thought about leaving so many times, and I even threatened to go more than once. But every time I did, he'd chain my heart with threats to harm himself if I left. He didn't just say it —he acted on it. Once, he climbed onto the window ledge, ready to jump.

I coaxed him back inside with promises I didn't want to make, but felt I had to. Another time, in a desperate tantrum, he smashed his head through a glass window. Each incident left me feeling trapped—emotionally shackled by his pain and my own fear of what he might do next.

I knew Kwame was sick, and all I wanted was to help him, to somehow make him whole again. I convinced myself that being there for him was my duty, that I couldn't abandon him when the world already had.

I wanted to be the one person who didn't give up on him. At least, that's what I kept telling myself—just as I imagine my mother once told herself the same thing. The truth, though, was harder to face: I had become as dependent on him as he was on me.

Fourteen

Kwame gave me a sense of worth by making me believe he needed me. I didn't grasp the long-term damage of staying in such a toxic relationship. In fact, I didn't even recognize it as abuse. To me, abuse had always meant physical violence because that's what I grew up seeing. No one ever explained that abuse could take many shapes—emotional, psychological, and beyond.

With my Section 8 voucher, I moved nearly every year, convinced that a change in environment might somehow help Kwame turn his life around. I clung to the hope that if I could just fix him, everything would fall into place. In my mind, our lives would magically transform into the fairy tale I so desperately wanted: he'd get a steady job, we'd get married, and all our struggles would fade away.

But it never worked. No matter where we went, he always found drugs. At the time, I used to say drugs found him, a notion so naïve it's almost laughable now. Drugs don't find people; people who want to get high find drugs. They'll sacrifice anything and everything to get them.

Case in point: shortly after we moved to the South Shore community, I thought we had finally turned a corner. I went grocery shopping and stocked up on enough food to last the entire month. Things seemed stable enough that I stopped re-bagging and hiding groceries—a survival tactic I had perfected over the years to protect our food. For the first few weeks, our new environment felt like the fresh start we desperately needed.

Kwame was doing odd jobs and bringing the money home, and I had a part-time job at a neighborhood burger joint. Together, we were raising our three small children, and for a fleeting moment, life felt almost normal. I allowed myself to believe that maybe, just maybe, we were on the right track.

But that illusion shattered when my best friend—who was babysitting for me—called in a panic while I was at work. Her voice trembled as she shouted into the phone that Kwame was in the kitchen, pulling food from the cabinets and the fridge and stuffing it all into garbage bags. I raced home as fast as I could, my heart pounding with dread.

By the time I arrived, he was gone—and so was most of our food. The fragile dream of a happily ever-after I'd clung to was crumbling before my eyes, leaving behind the bitter realization that some things might never change.

After years trapped in this endless cycle, now with three kids depending on me, I was desperate to break free from the toxic environment that had consumed my life. I turned to the only thing I could think of: prayer. But it didn't take long to realize that prayer alone wasn't enough. I couldn't just hope for a miracle—I had to take action.

I had to make a choice, both in my heart and in my mind, that I was ready to leave him. It wasn't an easy decision, but I finally understood a truth I had ignored for far too long: I couldn't save someone who was unwilling—or unable—to save himself. If I stayed, I wasn't just risking my happiness; I was sentencing myself and my children to a life of misery. And that was no longer an option.

I was too young to exist like that. I was twenty-one, but I felt like seventy-one. I should have been in college, pledging to join a sorority. I should have been living in a dorm room on campus, cramming for finals, preparing my thesis, and getting ready for graduation.

Instead, I had three children, all under the age of four, that I was trying to raise. I was tired most of the time, and all I wanted to do was sleep. I had grown weary of crying and trying to convince someone else of his worth, when all the time I wasn't realizing my own. I was tired of seeing my children hungry because their daddy couldn't control his habit and would sacrifice their meals to feed his addiction.

Because I was blinded by so-called love and misplaced loyalty, I didn't have the sense or fortitude to just walk away. I knew he would never voluntarily leave me alone, and I didn't have the inner strength to force him out. I had convinced myself that I was a victim and was in the predictable mode of waiting to be rescued. I'm thankful God understood my confusion, because it was divine intervention that set the stage for the events that followed.

I woke up early one Sunday morning to the uplifting sound of gospel music playing on the radio. Kwame had been out all night on one of his crack binges and hadn't returned. My brother and cousin were visiting for Christmas break, and the house was quiet.

Normally, I would get up, join them in the living room to watch music videos, and fix breakfast for my babies. But this morning, I stayed in bed. The song that stirred me awake was one of my favorites by Reverend James Cleveland, "I Don't Feel No Ways Tired."

"Nobody told me the road would be easy. I don't believe He brought me this far to leave me."

The lyrics touched my fatigued soul, soothing me back to sleep. Suddenly, I was jolted awake by a streak of fire bursting through the top of the closed bedroom door. My heart raced as I leapt out of bed. Disoriented, I opened the door to see what was happening—not realizing at the time how close I was to being burned alive.

Instead of flames, I was met by a wall of thick black smoke that hissed and crackled like a living thing. Still confused, I slammed the door shut as the smoke seeped into the room. I grabbed my babies from the bed and placed them gently on the floor, instinctively covering them with a blanket.

Frantically, I ran to the old, weathered window and tried to force it open, but it wouldn't budge. My first thought was to grab one of my son's glass baby bottles and break the pane, but I hesitated, worried about the landlord's reaction to a broken window.

At that moment, I still hadn't grasped the severity of the fire. It wasn't until I noticed the terrified faces of my neighbors, staring and pointing from the street below on the side of the building, that panic set in. Their expressions said it all: this was no small fire, and I needed to act fast.

Their screams of "Oh my God!" and "Somebody help them!" set my nerves into high gear, and I immediately began praying. I saw that my brother and cousin made it out because they were also outside, helplessly looking up at the window, their eyes wide with fear.

Within minutes, firemen were at our window, breaking through the glass and instructing me to pass my babies to them. When my last child was out and they pulled me to safety, they repeatedly yelled, "Good job, Mother. You kept the babies safe. Good job, Mother!"

I initially thought there was only smoke damage, perhaps from a grease fire in the kitchen, so I was confused by the firemen's enthusiastic praise for our survival. It wasn't until I was being placed in the ambulance that I looked back at the front of the house and saw the true extent of the fire. The place was an inferno, flames angrily pouring through the windows, leaping toward the top of the two-flat building and licking at the roof.

That was the moment it hit me just how blessed we were. Later, my brother and cousin described the fire to me, and their account sent a chill through my entire body. The blaze had consumed everything in the living room, swallowing furniture, walls, and belongings in its relentless flames. The fire left nothing behind but charred remains.

But the room where my children and I had been sleeping? It was untouched. Not a single thing in that room bore the mark of the inferno. It was as if an invisible shield had protected us from the devastation happening just beyond those walls. Even now, I can't fully explain it, but I know in my heart that it wasn't a coincidence. That untouched room was a testament to something greater than myself—a powerful reminder of grace in the midst of destruction.

The source of the fire was a faulty furnace, located just two steps from my bedroom. I had complained about it to the property owners before, but nothing had been done. Even now, I shudder to think about what could have happened if my door had been open—or worse, if one of my children had been walking past when it flared up.

The kids and I were admitted to the hospital for minor smoke inhalation, but most of the trauma we suffered was emotional. My children were so terrified that they cried out for me all night. Recognizing their fear, the nursing staff kindly crammed three large hospital cribs into my room so they could stay with me. I will forever be grateful for their compassion.

We lost everything in the fire, but our lives were spared. Kwame didn't even know where we were, only learning about the incident when he showed up at the house the day after. By then, Red Cross had put me and the children in a motel for the night, and afterward, we stayed with my mother until I found another apartment.

I recognized this as my chance to break free from Kwame and his addiction, to reclaim some semblance of peace and stability in my life. I knew that if I didn't get away, I would lose myself completely to the chaos that constantly lured me into his destructive world.

When I found a new apartment in the Chatham community, I moved in quickly, determined to start fresh. But even new surroundings couldn't shake the darkness that seemed to cling to me, following me no matter where I went.

Pushed into an emotional and psychological beat down by the instigation of past troubles in my mother's home, I was goaded into a fight that I was not prepared to handle. I was mousy, weak, and accepting of the worse. The stench of this dysfunction must have oozed from my pores, because even some so-called religious folk treated me like I was dirt.

The young couple who owned the apartment destroyed by the fire professed to be devout followers of a religion I won't name. Before the fire, they often tried to persuade me to join their faith, claiming that if I gave myself to the god they worshipped, all my problems would disappear.

The wife sanctimoniously held herself up as an example, proclaiming that I too, could achieve success like hers if I embraced their god. They even brought me their bible and encouraged me to read and live by its teachings. On the surface, their intentions seemed sincere, but their actions eventually revealed their true nature.

Two weeks after the fire—caused by their negligence in properly repairing the furnace (they had allowed a relative to work on it instead of hiring a professional)—a friend advised me to ask the wife if they might help with some of the small items I had lost, such as dishes. Their insurance would cover the loss of the building, but my children and I had nothing except a single day's worth of clothes donated by the Red Cross.

I called the wife from a payphone across the street from our new place, my fingers nervously dialing the number. My voice trembled as I stumbled through my request for help. I could imagine the disdain on her face when she curtly replied, "We can't help you. We lost our building. Why don't you just take your little aid check and go buy you some stuff?"

Those were her exact words, seared into my brain and tattooed on my heart. Her response made me feel like an insignificant bug begging for a handout.

All I could do was mumble a polite thank-you and then cry my eyes out after hanging up. I crossed the street in a daze as I headed home. I had expected more from someone who had presented herself as holier than thou while trying to recruit me into her religious fold.

Another lesson learned: people can only be the sum of who they truly are, regardless of their religious affiliation. It's the heart that shapes their moral compass and determines how they treat others.

In defense of her husband, he showed up at my new apartment two hours after that phone call with a sincere apology and an envelope containing two hundred dollars in cash. He explained his wife had told him about our conversation and that he felt ashamed. He also admitted that she didn't know he was coming to see me, let alone giving me the money.

I was deeply grateful for his kindness. It was the first time I had experienced such a heartfelt gesture from a man without a sexual ultimatum attached to it.

Before calling the landlords, out of desperation, I had gone by the two-flat to see if I could salvage any of our belongings. As I walked up the cold, dark hallway stairs, an immobilizing fear gripped me.

The soot-covered walls felt like they were closing in, and I was overwhelmed by a sense of malevolence in the building. Though I wasn't particularly religious, I felt something sinister there. I barely made it halfway up the stairs before the fear became too much, and I turned and ran out.

A few months later, out of curiosity, I passed by the house again. The couple had rebuilt the building with the insurance money they'd received, and it was stunning—like new. I guess their god did indeed bless them.

At the time, I had no furniture, no clothes, and no dishes

when I moved into my new apartment. But my God blessed me, too.

When the kids and I were being discharged from the hospital, I had met a woman who worked in the financial services department. While she was taking my medical card information for insurance purposes, she asked what had happened. I explained, and she listened with genuine concern. She took down my number and gave me hers, telling me to call if I ever needed anything.

I didn't have to call her. Ms. Taylor kept in touch with me, helping me find the new apartment and suggesting I call the previous landlords. She never belittled me, never talked down to me, and followed up every form of encouragement with action to support me. She was truly a godsend.

When I told her about the call to Mrs. Landlord, Ms. Taylor and another member of her congregation showed up at my door a few hours later with bags full of clothes, dishes, toys for the kids, and food—all donated by members of their church. Before leaving, they prayed with me and invited me to attend services, an invitation I humbly accepted.

After they left, I fed the kids, put them to bed, and began decorating my empty apartment with the gifts they brought. I cried as I hung up a red flower-patterned towel set in the bathroom. For the first time, I felt truly seen. Someone cared. They didn't see me as just a young single mother in trouble; they saw someone worth helping—not a person looking for a handout.

That's what I had craved so deeply: for someone to look past my situation and see the person I was beneath the layers of bad decisions and unfortunate circumstances. But not everyone is willing—or even capable—of doing that.

Thankfully, many of the congregants of South Shore Baptist Church, where Ms. Taylor and her friend attended and where my kids and I would later become members, did.

I will always be grateful to them for seeing the potential in me, for finding value where others saw none. But here's the thing: instead of waiting for someone to uncover the diamond in the rough, I should have been focused on finding my own inner jewel. I didn't understand this at the time—I didn't even know how to begin discovering—me. Like Sleeping Beauty, I was asleep to my own worth, waiting for something or someone to awaken it.

But God was already at work, whispering truths into my life. Through every trial, every mistake, and every heartache, He was opening my eyes. He was teaching me to pay attention to the lessons hidden in the details of my life, helping me glean wisdom from even the most painful experiences.

Those lessons weren't over—they were just beginning. The next phase of my journey taught me an essential truth: you can't run from your problems. Like shadows, they'll follow you wherever you go, growing larger the longer you avoid them. The only way to break free is to turn around, face them head-on, and resolve them. Otherwise, they'll always find you.

Fifteen

F or a few weeks after the fire, and with Kwame out of the picture, I could breathe again—somewhat. I focused on creating a sense of normalcy for the kids and myself. But as Christmas approached, a bittersweet ache settled in my chest. We had survived, but I couldn't afford to get my children any presents. The thought of disappointing them on such a special day broke my heart.

Then, as if heaven itself intervened again, Ms. Taylor and the church stepped in. They brought two large bags of gifts and even gave me a small sum of money. Their kindness continued to leave me speechless, tears brimming in my eyes as I thanked them over and over.

Determined to make Christmas memorable, I used the money to buy a tree. But instead of putting it up right away, I hid the gifts and the tree under my bed, planning to create a magical surprise.

On Christmas Eve, once the kids were asleep, I got to work. In the quiet of the night, I set up the tree, my hands trembling with emotion as I strung the lights and hung the ornaments. When I placed the star on top, tears spilled down my face. It wasn't just a Christmas tree—it was a symbol of hope, of survival, of better days to come.

I wrapped the presents in colorful paper, placing each one carefully beneath the glowing branches, and stepped back to take it all in. The living room was empty of furniture, but the soft glow of the tree filled it with warmth and love.

Early the next morning, I couldn't wait to see the kids' reactions. I woke them up and then led them into the living room. Their sleepy eyes widened with surprise and delight when they saw the tree. They tore into their gifts, giggling and squealing as they held up their treasures. For a brief moment, the struggles we had endured melted away, replaced by the pure magic of Christmas.

That day was a gift for me, too. Watching their joy reminded me why I fought so hard to keep going.

But that temporary peace didn't erase my fears. The first few weeks after our lives went up in flames were some of the hardest. I couldn't shake the feeling that Kwame might show up. Every sound at the door made my heart race. I would walk through the apartment, checking the locks, peeking into cabinets to make sure the food was still there. I had learned not to take anything for granted—not peace, not safety, not even a meal.

When it came time to go grocery shopping, I spent every dime I had, still haunted by the fear that any leftover money could be taken. Out in public, I constantly felt the weight of the world's eyes on me, judging me for being a young, poor, single mother. These feelings weren't rational—they were the lingering effects of dysfunctional conditioning. To move forward, I had to recognize that I was suffering from trauma and commit to addressing it.

The first step in reclaiming my life was confronting the very thing I had been running from. I knew that if I didn't face it head-on, it would haunt my every move. I just didn't expect it to happen so quickly.

Kwame was clever and manipulative—I'd learned that the hard way. But I had been careful. Only a handful of people knew where I lived, and I was confident no one would betray my trust. Yet somehow, he found me. When I pulled up to my building in Ms. Taylor's car, there he was, sitting on the stoop like he belonged there.

Ms. Taylor saw him too. "Do you want me to keep going?" she asked, her voice calm but full of concern.

I paused, my heart pounding, but it was too late. He had already spotted me. As he rose to his feet and started walking toward the car, I knew I couldn't avoid the confrontation any longer. It was time to face him.

In the trunk, I had a brand-new microwave that the church had purchased for the kids and me. I hesitated to bring it inside, afraid he would take it. But a voice inside me pushed back, firm and insistent: This is what you've been running from. You have to stop running, or he will never stop chasing. Face him. Face this dysfunction head-on.

I was done hiding. I was tired of living in fear, tired of worrying about what he might take from us next. So, I stood my ground. I confronted him, my voice steady even though my heart was racing. I told him he couldn't come to my home. For the first time in a long time, the kids and I had found a sense of stability, and I wasn't about to let him destroy that. In the back of my mind, I questioned God, "How could you have led him back to me?"

The answer dawned as soon as the question formed. Instead of walking away like a woman, I ran away like a victim. I had never ended things with him; I'd simply left without telling him it was over.

We can't assume that people—especially those struggling with their own demons—will understand our limits simply because we walk away. Yes, actions often speak louder than words, but sometimes the words are necessary too. We have to draw clear boundaries, and when we do, we must stand firm. The truth is, abusers—regardless of the form their abuse takes—only have the power we allow them to hold over our lives.

But I wasn't strong enough and my sense of control was just as fragile. I didn't want to completely shatter his heart, or maybe I was afraid that cutting ties would only provoke him to cling to me harder. After all, he'd found me and it was obvious I couldn't keep running.

So, instead of making a clean break, I tried to wean him off of us. I told him he needed to get help, and that until he was clean, it would be best if he didn't come around. It felt like a compromise, and deep down, I knew it wasn't enough.

I adapted to the situation the only way I knew how—by bargaining. I set flimsy rules to create some semblance of control; when he visited, he had to call first. If he didn't, the door would stay shut. It was a thin thread of a boundary, but it was all I could manage on the spot. He nodded, claimed he understood, and promised to do whatever I asked if it meant staying in our lives.

When he left with no further argument, I thought my plan worked. But like all his empty promises, it didn't last. After only a day or so, he showed up unannounced, ignoring everything I said. It was a harsh reminder of how weak my power was—and how much I still had to learn about reclaiming it.

True to my enabling nature, I succumbed to his pressure and opened the door, but I kept the gate locked between us, demanding to know why he didn't follow the rules. At least I was learning, because when he claimed he wanted to take the kids to the park, I stood my ground and refused to let him in. Naturally, he pretended to be upset and accused me of keeping his kids from him. Refusing to be drawn into that debate, I closed the door.

He cursed and kicked at the gate, calling me every dirty name in the book. Little did I know this would prove to be my biggest test. This lesson wasn't only for me; it was for him, as well. Although it was painful for both of us, the events that followed would essentially save his life.

Not more than ten minutes after I closed the door in his face, Kwame was in my home, having scaled the second floor like a black Spiderman. He used the air conditioning unit that was housed on the storefront beneath my apartment and climbed in through the window.

My heart dropped as I saw him emerging from an empty bedroom, a look of anger and determination on his face and in his stride. I felt like I was in a scary movie, running from the boogeyman as I tried to grab the kids and lock us in the bedroom.

He caught me before I could slam the door. When I looked into his eyes, all traces of the man I once loved were gone. I pleaded with him to take what he wanted from the house—

the microwave, the food—whatever it took to get him away from us.

For the first time, he didn't want any of those things. He wanted to punish me for leaving him behind. He didn't understand how I could just walk away from us—we were supposed to be a family. No amount of explaining would satisfy his anger.

His moment of insanity broke through even the worst drug craving when he ripped my nightgown off and raped me at knifepoint. I didn't fight him. I simply lay there and prayed it would end quickly. He ripped the phone off the wall afterward, tied me up with the cord and took off with our oldest daughter, who was only four or five at the time.

I was distraught, but I escaped my bindings and ran across the street, using the payphone to call the police. The officer who responded, a tall middle-aged Black man, was visibly upset when I described what happened, explaining I faked how tightly my hands were bound so Kwame would leave enough room for me to wiggle free.

With anger and compassion like that of a father, the officer encouraged me to file an order of protection and to press charges. I did so the next day. Within a few days, my daughter was back safely with me and Kwame was in jail.

For weeks after his arrest, he called relentlessly with the help of his public defender, begging me to drop the charges. I refused. Despite him being the father of my children and our years together, there was no erasing what he had done the last time we were face to face. What he did to me was, without question, the worst thing a man could do to a woman. Especially one who'd been traumatized by sexual assault as a child.

He insisted he wasn't himself, blaming years of drug abuse for his mental state. He pleaded, his voice heavy with desperation, for me to understand that he was sick. I understood. More than anyone else, I knew what was going on, and I even acknowledged his sickness, but it didn't change my decision. There was no excuse for what he had done. I advised him to focus on getting help while he was behind bars.

No amount of love or promises could make me drop the charges. I knew better. As a teenager with my stepfather, I had seen firsthand that a brief stint in jail doesn't bring recovery. He needed real help, and my children and I needed peace. This wasn't just about me—it was about protecting them, too.

This was my first real step toward progress.

I was slowly blossoming into the woman I needed to become, learning to navigate the obstacles and barriers I had placed in my own way with my past decisions. I loved this newfound strength, but it scared me at first. I wasn't used to taking a firm stand.

Testifying against him in court wasn't easy. I wrestled with myself, questioning if I was doing the right thing. After all, we had endured so much together before his decline. He had stood by me when my stepfather made my life unbearable. The weight of that history clashed with the reality of what he'd done, creating an emotional storm that was hard, but not impossible, to weather.

The most difficult thing to do is to go against our hearts. What makes it easier is when we use our heads and allow commonsense to prevail. I had to weigh the options: drop the charges and continue to believe that love would fix him. That would only lead to me running away again and living in fear.

Or, face the truth of what happened to me and hold him accountable for his actions.

Weighing the options also meant understanding the outcome of the decision I was making. It was unrealistic to expect that our love would be enough to change him. If that were the case, love would have been enough to stop him from going over the edge.

Holding him accountable for the criminal act of rape meant he would have to pay for his crime, and that would get him off the streets. It would be up to him after that to decide his path: succumb to the elements many fell to behind bars or get the help he claimed he wanted by facing his own demons.

Even his public defender was surprised I was going through with it. Most women, no matter the frequency or severity of the abuse, don't take the stand against their partners. Defiantly, I testified before the judge, recounting the ordeal as Kwame sat at the defense table, watching me.

When I was excused from the stand, I walked out of the courtroom and broke down. The decision hadn't been easy, but it was necessary—for me, for my children, and for the future I was carving out of the wreckage of my tortured life.

Later that night, the prosecutor called to inform me that Kwame had been found guilty and sentenced to ten years in prison. He thanked me for my cooperation, acknowledging how rare it was for someone to testify against the father of their children.

I felt a sense of relief—not vindictive satisfaction, but a quiet release. I held no malice toward Kwame. In fact, I still loved him. But I also knew he was sick, and I understood how slim the chances were that he would voluntarily enter and stick with a rehab program.

My relief wasn't just about his conviction; it was about reclaiming my freedom. I no longer wanted to be a prisoner of the dysfunction that had plagued my life. Yet, despite the enormity of what I had endured—the rape, the mental abuse tied to his addiction, and the countless other traumas—I never sought counseling. I thought I could simply move on, start fresh, and leave the past behind.

That was a mistake.

As I would later come to understand, it's nearly impossible to start anew without first addressing the deep wounds left by trauma. Moving forward requires recognizing that we, too, are affected by what we've experienced, and it takes courage to seek help to heal those scars.

Statistics highlight just how challenging this journey can be for victims. Studies show that less than 20% of sexual assault survivors seek professional counseling or support services, even though therapy has been proven to aid in emotional recovery.

For survivors like me, shame, stigma, and the urge to simply "move on" often keep us silent. But untreated trauma doesn't disappear—it lingers, manifesting in devastating ways like depression, anxiety, and difficulty forming healthy relationships.

All of these challenges were waiting for me as I entered the next phase of my life.

Sixteen

There has to be a reason nature chose women to bear life. Why didn't it share the responsibility between men and women? Why are women the ones who go through the cycles of menstruation, the challenges of pregnancy, and the intense pain of childbirth? What made nature decide that this incredible, exhausting, and transformative role should be ours?

When you think about how perfect the world works—the Earth's rotation, gravity, the delicate balance of ecosystems—it's clear that everything has a purpose. Women's role in creating and nurturing life is no different. Our bodies were designed for this, not as a punishment, but as a reflection of the strength and courage we carry.

We are built to adapt, endure, and recover in ways that are nothing short of miraculous. But it's not just the physical strength—it's the emotional resilience, the innate ability to nurture, and the persistence to keep going no matter the odds.

It's no wonder the women in fairy tales were always written to find a way, no matter what challenges stood in their path. The stories Mama told me all shared one common thread: the women were strong and determined, whether they were escaping danger, outsmarting their enemies, or rising above impossible odds.

Yes, it's exhausting. Yes, there are moments when we wish we could pass this responsibility off for a day—or forever. But when you take a step back, it's clear that this role is about more than the pain and challenges. It's about growth, transformation, and the quiet power that's been within us all along, like Dorothy discovering her strength with those pretty ruby slippers.

Nature didn't choose women by accident. It saw something in us we often forget ourselves—an incredible ability to create, cultivate, and overcome. That's not just biology. That's a gift.

Whatever the reasons, this extraordinary gift demands respect. Just as men possess physical strength, traditionally associated with protection and provision, and receive respect for the role they play, so too should the life-giving power of women command reverence.

Yet, somewhere along the way, the sanctity of womanhood has been devalued and denigrated by both men and women alike. The causes of this erosion are topics of debate. Some argue that one gender bears more responsibility than the other, but blame does little to repair what's been lost.

As women, it is up to us to restore the value of womanhood to its rightful place. The reclamation of respect for who we are and what we bring into the world must begin with us.

One of the most valuable lessons my mother taught me was to avoid focusing on the big picture right away when searching for answers. Instead, she encouraged me to start small—by looking inward and examining things on a personal level before considering the external factors. Perhaps this approach is a recipe for personal growth that we can all benefit from.

Genuine change begins with individual self-assessment and action. Once we've done the inner work, we can broaden our perspective and tackle the bigger picture with clarity and purpose.

Many of us grew up hearing that we were damsels in need of rescue, relying on Prince Charming or a knight to save us from the monsters of the world—presumably because of their strength. Fairy tales often ended with the same promise: they lived happily ever after. But not all stories fit this mold. Some featured women who took matters into their own hands, like Goldilocks.

I'll share it with you the way Mama told it to me (with my own little flair, of course). Goldilocks, who had wandered into the woods by herself and ended up lost, stumbled upon a cozy little house and knocked on the door. When no one answered, she let herself in.

When she smelled food, she realized she was hungry. Spying three bowls of porridge on the kitchen table, she didn't hesitate. She sampled the first bowl—it was too hot! The second bowl was way too cold. But that third bowl? Chef's kiss. She polished it off without a second thought, thinking, someone in this house knows how to season.

Satisfied, but now feeling a little tired from all the forest trekking, she ventured into the living room. There were three chairs, so she decided to cop a squat. The first one was like sitting on a slab of wood—that was a hard pass. The second chair was too soft—like trying to sit on a marshmallow.

But the third one was perfection. She leaned back, stretched out her legs, and snap! It collapsed under her. So much for quality craftsmanship, she thought, brushing herself off.

With her hunger handled and her attempt at relaxation a total fail, she decided she needed to sleep off the day. Upstairs, she found three beds, fully made as if they were waiting for her. The first one was stiff as a board. The second one was so soft it felt like she was sinking into quicksand. But that third was just right. She climbed in, snuggled up, and fell fast asleep.

Meanwhile, the three little bears, who were the owners of the cottage, came home and were not thrilled when they saw their food tampered with and their furniture broken.

They made their way to the bedroom and found Goldilocks curled up, snoring peacefully in Baby Bear's bed. They awakened her, and when she saw them, the frightened girl sprang up like a jack-in-the-box. She bolted straight out of the house and into the woods, never to be seen by the Bear family again.

There was no Prince Charming waiting for her as she ran out the door; there was no knight waiting to whisk her away from danger. She got out of there by herself and presumably lived happily ever after.

Goldilocks represented independence and learned wisdom. She got into a mess on her own by venturing into an unfamiliar place without knowing what to expect. When she discovered she may be in danger, she didn't hesitate—she made the decision to save herself.

As women, we are bound to make mistakes in life. We will venture into the unknown, experimenting and trying different things until we discover what suits us. Along the way, we may even make poor choices—some with significant consequences.

But we also possess the strength and resilience to recover. We don't need to be rescued.

When little girls are taught that women always need to be saved, we fail to equip them to stand up and face challenges on their own. For years, I prayed for a gallant knight to ride in and rescue me from the chaos of my life. What I didn't realize was that I had been the rescuer all along. I was the one helping, enduring, and taking care of others—while I sat there hoping, waiting, and wishing for someone to save me.

Had I paid closer attention, I would have realized I was capable of saving myself. Better yet, I could have avoided many of the traps I fell into by not attempting to rescue others. Not that I should have stopped helping people—I would never do that. But I've learned there are limits to what I can do, and those limits are essential to my own survival.

The biggest limit? Establishing boundaries. A drowning person who cries out for help can easily pull us under if their weight is too much for us to bear. Before rushing in to save someone else, we have to ensure we're equipped to handle the situation. Otherwise, we risk losing ourselves in the process.

If we see we can't handle the challenge, we need to seek help or find alternative solutions. It's not wise to always throw ourselves into someone else's problems, because we could end up drowning right along with that person. This applies to lovers, spouses, children, friends, and family.

I learned this from my mother. The strength I saw in her over the years is a testament to the woman she grew to become and who she tried to empower others to be. She knew the difference between helping others and trying to save them.

The early decisions she made and the life she led were not easy because she made many mistakes along the way. She learned from her missteps and attempted to pay it forward by advocating for and educating others. She also knew when to step back and let them work things out for themselves.

This is how she became my greatest teacher. As I look back at her journey, I have a level of respect for her that surpasses the misguided animosity I once held in my heart that was fueled by ignorance. I didn't understand the hardship of being a woman in a society that has little patience for those who get lost along the way.

I scratched and clawed my way from the bottom of the cesspool and walked through dark forests as I tried to figure life out. I can still see her expression as she would say to me, "You'll know when you've had enough." What sounds like a redundant cliché turned out to be the most poignant piece of advice she gave me because it would apply to every area of my life.

The months that followed the so-called freedom from my children's father were heavy. The guilt of sending him to prison coupled with sadness because my life was at a standstill continued to rattle me.

I could hear the echo of my stepfather's words; "You ain't shit ... you ain't never gonna be shit." Double negatives aside, his words seemed prophetic.

By the time I was twenty-one, I was single with three small children, had no job and no viable education. I was a living, walking, breathing stereotype. I felt like I was being criticized everywhere I went. The truth is, I was judging myself.

I didn't feel worthy of anything or anyone with any sense of value and decency. Therefore, I found myself involved in meaningless flings with men who gave less than a damn about me just so I could satisfy some internal need to feel wanted.

The relationship that felt just right and took off into something more serious was with the man who would become my first husband. We dated off and on for two years, and I gave birth to our son shortly after we wed. While we were dating, we both knew I was mentally and emotionally lost.

He was looking for someone to save, and I was looking to be rescued. I knew I wanted something, but had no clue what that was. I assumed marriage was the key to identifying that desire and would bring the stability I needed. I quickly learned how wrong I was.

Maturity is a process that can induce a lot of growing pains. Because I didn't recognize the value in learning about true love and what that emotional tangent felt like, my marriage lasted only a year. Instead of acknowledging this mistake right away, I looked for any excuse to justify its end.

The simple truth is I wasn't ready to get married and shouldn't have rebounded into another relationship until I dealt with the issues that haunted me. Because I didn't take those steps, subsequent relationships would be just as chaotic.

I became an emotional bag lady. I had a lot of baggage in my life, and before I could empty the previous garbage (low self-esteem, molestation, guilt, shame, depression, and abuse), I added more drama. Eventually, my bag overflowed, slowing and weighing me down, stalling any progress to the finish line of personal achievement.

By the time I turned twenty-four, I was a divorcee with four young children. However, the changes in my life were coming in waves. I was growing, blossoming into the rose that I was meant to become. It was not a smooth transition. During those years of trying to climb upward, I battled with a lot of demons as my past merged with the present, trying to shape a path that would lead to a promising future.

Early on, I recognized the cycles that were being repeated and saw the pattern of abuse, and I grew concerned for my children. I knew if I didn't break the cycles, they would follow in my footsteps and could pass the same dysfunction down to their children. The years forward were not perfect; however, things were getting better, which meant I was making progress.

That's an important step in anyone's life. If you can see yourself doing better, no matter how long it takes, then you're on the right track. Progress is an individual thing that should not be measured by anyone else's standard. Understand who you are and where you want to be. Then set your goals accordingly. If you meet the standards you set for yourself, then you are succeeding.

The summer after my last ordeal with Kwame, I decided it was time to take control of my destiny. I signed up for the GED test and passed it on the first try. While I was proud of the achievement, it didn't completely erase the regret I felt for not walking across the stage and earning my high school diploma. Still, it was a significant step forward.

By the time I was twenty-three, I had landed a career in social services—my first salaried job. A few years later, following my passion for writing, I wrote and self-published my first book. I was making moves and finally beginning to shape the future I had dreamed of.

There was still one major issue I needed to address. Until I did so, I remained in chains, emotionally bound because of the one thing I was searching for but didn't realize I possessed all the time; the ability to love myself.

Seventeen

I loved when Mama told the story of the three little pigs and their nemesis, the big bad wolf. According to the tale, whenever the pigs built a house, the wolf would come along to huff … and puff … and blow it down.

The first house was made of straw. The wolf came and blew it down with ease. The second house was built out of wood. The wolf had to work a little harder, but it too gave way and toppled. Finally, the pigs learned from their past failures and built their house out of brick. This time, the wolf's huffs and puffs were in vain, and the house stood firm.

That's exactly how life felt for me as I started adulting. Every time I took steps forward, something seemed to come along and knock me back. At first, I tried building a life on a flimsy foundation made of straw (instincts). When I left my mother's home and built my world with Kwame, his drug abuse and dysfunction came like the wolf and blew it all away.

Next, I tried building on a foundation made of wood (faith).

It was stronger than straw, but still not resilient enough to withstand the winds of chaos.

Finally, having learned from my experiences, I started building my world on a foundation made of brick (faith plus works). Faith alone wasn't enough; I realized I needed to use the tools God had given me and put in the effort to move forward.

The moral of my story seemed clear: no matter how much wind came against me, no matter how fiercely the big bad wolf huffed ... and puffed ... my house would stand up to the harshest of winds.

But that's how life works in fairy tales. Reality, as I soon discovered, is far more complicated.

Even though I was making strides in life, I still couldn't seem to get it right when it came to love. I wasn't the same naïve little girl blindly walking through life, but somehow, I kept falling into the same messy relationship patterns. Why did I keep repeating the same mistakes? Why couldn't I get it right?

After my divorce from my first husband, I wasn't ready to face the world on my own. It's human nature to crave companionship. But sometimes, because of that longing, we excuse behaviors and overlook red flags. What I didn't realize at the time was that a partner who adds to your burdens instead of sharing them isn't a helpmate—they're a hindrance.

It wasn't until I was in my thirties that this truth finally clicked. By then, heartache had knocked me down enough times to force me to pay attention. I had to confront an uncomfortable reality: I was choosing partners who reflected my own wounds and unresolved issues. This isn't uncommon. Studies reveal that age plays a significant role in relationship choices.

According to research from the National Longitudinal Study of Adolescent to Adult Health, individuals in their twenties are more likely to make impulsive, emotionally driven relationship decisions, often influenced by past trauma or unmet needs. By our thirties, many of us begin to seek more stability and accountability in our relationships—but only if we've done the work to address our personal baggage.

Here's a hard truth: if we don't take the time to examine our choices, to figure out why we're drawn to the same harmful patterns, we'll just keep running in circles. We'll hop from one relationship to the next, replacing one form of heartbreak with another, convincing ourselves that the next one will be different—without ever changing anything about how we choose.

It took heartbreaking situations and eventually a broken heart before I finally confronted the common thread in all of it: me. Not in a self-blaming way, but in a manner that forced me to take accountability for my choices. I couldn't fix what I wouldn't face, and I couldn't grow until I was willing to do the hard work of looking inward.

Whenever I wasn't in a relationship, I craved intimate love and assumed it was simply because I was alone. In one sense, I was right—I was missing love. But it wasn't the love another person could provide. What I lacked was the love I needed to have for myself. Until I learned to establish that, the last thing I needed was a man in my life.

The instinct to pair up with someone is natural, but my problem was that it had become a necessity. I believed I needed someone in my life to feel balanced. Like my mother, I was searching for a partner to make me feel complete. And, truthfully, I loved the sensation of falling in love.

It's interesting how falling in love has a way of showing us only the good in someone. Even when we catch a glimpse of the red flags, we ignore them, choosing instead to hold on to the euphoria. For every relationship that turned out to be a disaster, the warning signs were always there from the start. But I made a conscious choice to ignore them, driven by my desire for companionship. Every time, the very thing I overlooked came back to bite me. Hard.

A wise soul once said, "When you see crazy comin', cross the street to the other side." The problem is, sometimes crazy is dressed up so well, it looks downright irresistible. If we don't take the time to look past the outer shell and truly see a person for who they are, we risk missing the signs altogether.

My "crazy" came in a sharp suit. He was handsome, older, intelligent, and boy, could he sing! His charm was magnetic. After several deep conversations, I was drawn to the similarities in our goals, and before long, we started dating. It wasn't long before dating turned into him moving in.

But as time went on, the cracks in his carefully polished exterior began to show. It became painfully clear that neither I nor my children were better off with him in our lives. In fact, his presence compounded the unresolved issues I was already struggling with, adding a whole new set of challenges. It turned out he was battling manic depression, alongside addictions to gambling and heroin.

I didn't know any of this at the beginning—because I hadn't asked the kinds of questions that might have revealed it. After all, who starts a budding relationship by asking, "Do you have a psychological disorder?" But looking back, maybe we should ask those questions! It might save a lot of heartache down the line.

The truth is, the thrill of falling for someone—and having them fall for us—often overshadows practicality. Nothing deflates the euphoria of romance faster than pulling out a questionnaire about mental health history.

Over time, I learned the value of paying attention to the little things about a person and using those observations to assess their overall character. Too often, we focus solely on their positive traits and dismiss red flags as "minor." Funny how those "minor" issues have a way of climbing to the top of the list of major problems when the relationship goes south.

I should have recognized this pattern from my past relationships. That's the beauty of life, though—we live, and hopefully, we learn. Some of us don't get it on the first try, and others need even more mistakes before it clicks. But no matter when the lesson finally lands, as long as we learn, there's room to grow. The downside of learning late, however, is that it can lead to stressful situations that take years to unravel—especially when shacking up is involved.

Why do we always let them move in?

That should have been a hard no—especially with children in the picture. But growing up, I saw this pattern repeated by nearly every single woman I knew. "Playing house," as the preachers called it, seemed normal, even logical. It was the default next step in relationships, no matter how ill-advised.

While I watched my children carefully, I was still making a dangerous choice by allowing someone into our lives without the sanctity of time to fully vet them. I got lucky, but that doesn't excuse the fact that I was repeating the same mistakes my mother made. What happened to me as a child and teenager could just as easily have happened to my children.

I thought I was making better choices in men. This one had a decent-paying job. At first. Yet even though he lived with us, ate with us, and enjoyed every comfort of my home, he eventually stopped contributing financially.

When he stopped pulling his weight and became a deadbeat, it was time to go. I was raising four young children—I would not have a grown, able-bodied man in my home who was not contributing, while I worked my ass off. But of course, there was drama. Because when you let someone move in, it's easy to get them through the door, but it can be hard as hell to get them out.

He pulled out every tool he could think of to bargain his way into staying. Once I discovered the truth about his addictions, which he had been clever at hiding, there was nothing he could do or say. From experience, I knew I couldn't help someone with a drug problem if they weren't ready to help themselves. When bargaining failed, he turned to fear and intimidation.

Kicking him out wasn't without consequences. He stalked me afterward, and I had to go to court to get an order of protection. Yes, I did the right thing in the end. But had I been more discerning and selective in the beginning, I wouldn't have wasted four years of my life in such a toxic situation.

Time is too precious. We should never underestimate its value by allowing ourselves to stay in unhealthy environments. Before we know it, days turn into months, and months into years. And I had to stop carrying the burdens of others on my back. I wish I'd learned this lesson earlier, because all that late learning nearly destroyed me—financially, emotionally, and spiritually—for years to come.

Why do we stay? What compels us to wake up every day in the same emotional chaos, sometimes for years at a time? Perhaps it's the maternal instinct that drives us to take care of others, no matter the cost. I watched my mother—and so many other women—cater to, take care of, and stand by their mates, no matter the pain those partners caused. And I became just like them.

I didn't view the men I was involved with in the same independent light I instilled in my children. Instead, I convinced myself they needed me to help them through their issues. So, I suffered alongside them, clinging to a misguided sense of pride that I was a so-called "good woman."

Maybe that's why I was always the rescuer. No matter how many times I fell, I forced myself to get back up and try again. But I wasn't attracting that kind of man. It wasn't until I readjusted my focus that I attracted the right partner.

Although I survived a drug addict, grew up and moved on from a rebound relationship-turned marriage, and then made it out alive from a manic-depressed, drug-addicted gambler, there was still one very important lesson I needed to learn about relationships; one that taught me the most about myself.

Eighteen

By the time I hit my early thirties, I had a clearer sense of what stability in a partner looked like. It meant they worked as hard as I did, didn't expect me to support them, he wasn't trying to move in right away, and—best of all —they didn't do drugs and only drank socially.

Bingo! I thought I'd finally cracked the code.

But life has a way of humbling you. He's the one who broke my heart. And at the same time, he became my greatest teacher in the school of hard knocks.

For a long time, I blamed him entirely for my broken heart. But when I took a hard, honest look inward, I realized a painful truth: he couldn't do anything to me that I didn't give him permission to do.

Let me explain. Before I met my current husband, I was deeply in love with a habitual cheater. In the beginning, I had no reason to suspect his unfaithfulness. He had so many wonderful qualities that I thought I'd hit the lover's lotto. I didn't feel the need to question him—or our relationship.

We spent a lot of time together, and to me, that was proof enough of his commitment. Besides, I was living by the advice I often gave my friends: don't go looking for trouble in a relationship. If something's wrong, trouble will find you eventually.

After four years, Ms. Trouble—aka the woman he had been seeing behind my back—found me. She called and politely informed me she had been dating him for over two years. I was stunned, yet oddly amused. He had hidden his indiscretions so well. Later, I would learn that his rabbit hole of lies ran even deeper than I imagined.

When I confronted him, we went through the familiar "let's make it work" routine. I convinced myself he had learned a valuable lesson and was ready to be with me and only me. Notice my phrasing: I convinced myself. He didn't fool me—I fooled myself because I wanted so desperately to believe it.

I wasn't alone in this cycle of self-deception. Studies show that over 50% of women who discover their partner has cheated choose to stay and try to repair the relationship. The reasons vary—from emotional attachment to financial dependency or simply believing in second chances. But forgiveness without accountability often leads to repeating the same mistakes.

He begged and pleaded for me to stay, swearing this time would be different. I chose to believe him. I stayed, clinging to the hope that this was his first and only time. Even when he continued cheating, I held on, praying for God to open his eyes so he could see our relationship the way I did.

Part of me didn't want to let go because this was my first genuine relationship that wasn't overshadowed by addiction or other glaring issues. He wasn't a deadbeat, he didn't use drugs, and he wasn't violent. He was diligent, a southern gentleman, and highly educated. I thought I had finally found my Prince Charming.

The combination of these qualities made me believe I had struck gold, and I didn't want to lose that. I convinced myself that staying and working things out was worth it, that love alone would win in the end.

But eventually, a moment of clarity broke through the fog. The truth was undeniable: the person who needed to change wasn't him—it was me.

He was exactly who he wanted to be—a man comfortable living a double life, splitting his time and affection between multiple women. He wasn't seeking change or struggling with who he was, so why was I praying for him to become someone he wasn't ready to be? That realization was painful, but also freeing.

If he wasn't ready to be faithful, it wasn't my place to wait or hope. It was my responsibility to leave, because his actions weren't just hurting me—they were reshaping me in ways I didn't want. I wasn't built to be the other woman, and I wasn't interested in sharing the man I loved. I deserved to be someone's priority. Despite what I'd gone through in my past, I was worthy of love and respect.

That is the moment I finally learned to choose myself.

The first time I caught him cheating should have been the end. He had proven that he couldn't be faithful, but I ignored the proof, telling myself I'd invested too much time to walk away. I held on, thinking he was a step up from the men I'd been with before, and that had to mean something. But all it really meant was that I was ignoring my own value.

I gave him a license to hurt me by forgiving him every time he got caught. I argued, cried, and sent him on guilt trips that worked—for a little while. But as soon as the dust settled, he went right back to what he knew. Cheating wasn't an accident for him; it was his way of life.

The problem wasn't just him, though—it was me believing I needed to change him. I clung to the idea that love alone would make him realize what we could have together. But love without respect, integrity, and accountability is hollow. And by the time I understood that, I had wasted almost seven years of my life waiting for someone who wasn't worthy of me.

There must be a level of ego tripping that comes from knowing you can get away with infidelity—when several people tolerate you jumping from one bed to another and still stick by you. My ex thrived on that power. His friends thought he was "the man" for pulling it off as long as he did.

Men like him often label women like me as "good women" because we don't give up easily. But what does that really mean? Does being a "good woman" mean enduring emotional hell while the person causing you pain continues to indulge in their selfish behavior? That's not good—it's naïve. Some might even call it foolish.

This doesn't mean we should walk away at the first sign of trouble. That's where discernment comes in. If we choose to stay and work through challenges, we must establish boundaries. We have to decide where the line is drawn, at what point we'll say, enough is enough.

And we need to communicate those boundaries upfront. We can't assume someone will automatically know our limits, nor can we expect them to respect boundaries we haven't set. Communication isn't just for their benefit—it's for our own affirmation. Saying it out loud reinforces our intentions and reminds us to stand firm when things get tough.

Yes, I was a good woman. I am a good woman. But not because I suffered his betrayal or stuck around through endless cycles of heartbreak. My worth doesn't come from how much pain I can endure. My value lies in my strength, my loyalty, and my independence.

I ended that relationship as a stronger, more confident woman. But not before I went through immense emotional agony. That heartbreak, however, became my salvation. It forced me to confront hard truths about myself and begin a journey of self-transformation.

He was my deepest heartache, but he was also my most valuable lesson.

Through the pain, I grew in ways I didn't know were possible. That growth gave me the strength to finally take control of my emotional and mental state. It forced me to look inward, something I'd avoided for far too long.

I thought something was wrong with me. His infidelity triggered old insecurities, and I began to believe I was undeserving of a good man. But the truth was, I didn't fully understand what a "good man" even was.

He wasn't a good man. Yes, he had some of the external qualities: a decent job, good manners, hardworking. Those traits might make someone a good catch, but it doesn't make them a good man. What truly matters are the internal qualities —integrity, loyalty, accountability. He lacked those, and it made all the difference.

When I finally turned my focus inward, I stopped asking, what's wrong with me? And started discovering what was right with me. That internal reflection allowed me to bloom like a rose breaking through the concrete.

I finally understood the real reason I hated being alone—it wasn't about craving the euphoria of falling in love. I hated being alone because I didn't like who I was. Keeping someone in my life, no matter how toxic, was a distraction. It let me avoid focusing on myself. After all, who wants to face their own flaws when they can bury them in someone else's drama?

But I couldn't live like that anymore.

There was too much I wanted to accomplish, too much life I hadn't yet experienced. The only way forward was to redirect my focus inward. When I did, I began identifying my issues and tearing down the walls I had built to hide them.

Armed with the hammer of truth, I came to terms with who I was: not perfect, not flawless, but certainly not damaged goods. I realized I didn't have to settle for less than I deserved —not in love, not in life, not in anything.

The greatest revelation came with this truth: I am not a victim. Not of circumstances, not of love. My happiness doesn't rest in the hands of my children, my husband, my friends, or my family. They can add to it, sure, but they don't control it. That responsibility is mine, and mine alone.

When I listen to the stories of other women—many my age or older—I'm often struck by the things that continue to derail their happiness. It's not their struggles that amaze me—life is full of struggles. What moves me is how some of us can live so long without learning when or how to put the brakes on our own misery.

The truth is, we rarely learn these lessons as teenagers. Those years are for coming of age: our first heartbreaks, figuring out who we are, and deciding what we want out of life. The harder lessons—like taking control of our own happiness—only come with time, experience, and a little self-reflection.

No, we can't go back and rewrite the chapters of our past. But we can choose to make our futures better. Taking control of our lives, of our happiness, isn't easy. It feels overwhelming at first, especially when the world around us feels unstable.

But it's necessary. If we want genuine success—if we want peace, freedom, and emotional independence—we have to take control.

It took me thirty-six years to figure it out, to make better choices for myself and in relationships. But once I did, the floodgates opened, and blessings poured in like I had never imagined.

Nineteen

W hen I was ten, my mother used to receive the Publishing House contest mailers and, like many others who hoped their ship would come in, she believed the hype that was hidden under the gold scratch-offs.

I'll never forget the happiness of that moment when she sat cross-legged on the bed with all the papers spread out in front of her and pulled out the one document that said she was the winner of all seven prizes! This included a car, some other items like furs and jewelry, and most important—cash!

We celebrated because this was the answer to our prayers. She could move us into an apartment with a bathroom, and I could finally have a bedroom of my own outside of the kitchen. She couldn't drive, but that didn't matter. We were taking the car anyway! So, she licked all the stamps for the magazines she had to purchase and put the winning imprints in the right place. It was a happy day.

Later that evening, as I was marveling over the winning documents, a fight broke out in the hallway of our building. Somehow, one of my uncles got caught up in the battle. Before long, the police showed up, and he found himself in a full-blown brawl with eight officers who battered him with their fists and batons.

It was a chaotic scene, as my mother was ready to jump into the fray to defend her brother but was being held back by her friends. I screamed as loud as my little voice could go and, in my anger, threw the Publisher's Clearing House papers I held in my hand at the officers who were pounding my uncle to a pulp. The situation was over within a few minutes, and my uncle was hauled off to jail.

I later found the papers that could have been our golden ticket out of the ghetto, soaked in a dirty mop bucket. I was devastated. It was that day I started to believe when good things happened, something bad would come along to counter it.

It seemed to be a pattern, as if luck was mocking us. My mother losing the love of her life to a motorcycle accident, her having a seizure in front of her date and it chasing him away, and other equally negative things just seemed to validate my pessimistic outlook.

When I got older, I understood there was no magic envelope filled with riches. There were only marketing schemes to sell magazines. More importantly, I understood that life is filled with both good and bad events, sometimes happening simultaneously. The bad just feels worse.

I'm a breathing, walking example of life's duality. As the new generation says, life just kept life'ing. Every time I thought I was getting ahead, something would happen to knock me two steps back. I'd look at my circumstances and wonder, "Why can't I ever catch a break?" It felt like I was cursed, like some unseen force was out to sabotage any progress I made.

That old saying, "When it rains, it pours," wasn't just a phrase to me—it was my reality. Before I found a strong support system in my husband, every setback felt like a personal attack. I'd celebrate a little win—like paying off a bill or finally getting caught up on rent—only to have some new disaster strike. The brakes on the car would go out, or something else equally vital would pop up, and I'd be back at square one, scrambling to stay afloat.

And that's the thing about life's curveballs—they don't come with warnings or a chance to prepare. They pile up, one after another, until you feel like you're carrying the weight of the world on your shoulders.

Stress is insidious like that. It sneaks up on you, settling in until it feels normal to be on edge, barely holding it together. For single mothers, that weight can be absolutely crushing. Juggling debt, raising kids, managing toxic relationships, and facing the relentless demands of life—it's no wonder I always felt like I was drowning.

If you're a single mom, you know what I'm talking about. The days are long, the nights are restless, and the list of responsibilities feels never-ending. According to the American Psychological Association, single parents experience significantly higher stress levels than most, with nearly 70% citing financial worries, childcare, and emotional exhaustion as daily struggles.

And when stress doesn't let up, it doesn't just wear you down mentally—it can show up in your body, too, leading to fatigue, anxiety, and even physical health problems.

The truth is, most of the stressful events in my life weren't random. They didn't come out of nowhere like some unlucky streak of bad timing. Many of those moments were the result of choices I made—or didn't make—and unresolved circumstances that snowballed.

When the lights or gas were shut off, it wasn't because the utility company had it out for me—it was because I hadn't paid the bill in months. When my car was repossessed in the dead of night, it wasn't some fluke—it was because I missed too many payments. And when my paycheck was garnished, it wasn't personal—it was because of debts I couldn't afford to pay off.

Did those moments feel overwhelming? Absolutely. But you know what I've learned? None of it made me a bad person. It made me human. We all make mistakes. Sometimes we're just trying to survive.

Life doesn't always give us straightforward choices. There were times I had to pick between paying a bill and feeding my kids and let me tell you—that's not a decision anyone should have to make. When you're constantly stuck between a rock and a hard place, the frustration can be devastating, piling up like bricks, one after another, until you feel completely walled in.

I know what it feels like to want to throw up your hands and give up, to feel like no matter what you do, it's never enough. When stress piles on, it's easy to focus on everything that's going wrong and completely overlook the things you're doing right. But here's the truth: even on the hardest days, you're showing up. You're making decisions. You're doing the best you can with what you have—and that's no small feat.

Realizing this helped me shift my perspective. I stopped seeing my struggles as curses and started understanding them as challenges I could tackle, step by step. It wasn't easy, and it didn't happen overnight, but bit by bit, I took back control. I stopped letting stress define me and started finding ways to chip away at the walls it built around me.

If you're feeling overwhelmed, know this: you're not alone. Stress may be heavy, but it doesn't have to crush you. You have the power to take control, even if it's just one small step at a time.

It's also important to stay mindful of the walls we unintentionally build in our lives—whether it's in relationships, finances, or how we approach decision-making. One thing always leads to another, and ignoring those issues won't make them go away. Problems have a way of catching up to us if we let them pile up. But when we face them head-on, we begin to see every wall can come down, one brick at a time.

Here are examples of how I unknowingly built walls around my life—barriers shaped by the choices I made and my responses to life's challenges:

Wall One: As a pregnant teenager, I faced overwhelming obstacles. After moving out of my mother's house, my daily commute to school from the north side of Chicago became grueling. Morning sickness, coupled with the long journey, wore me down. It all became too much, and I stopped going to school, promising myself I'd return in the summer after the baby was born.

That summer never came. Living on my own and making my own rules pushed school further down my list of priorities. Dropping out closed doors I didn't fully understand at the time, limiting my opportunities and narrowing my options for years.

Wall Two: Determined to catch up, I earned my GED and eventually enrolled in college. But by then, I was raising four children, working full-time, attending school full time, and clinging to a dysfunctional relationship with a habitual cheater. My plate wasn't just full—it was overflowing. Then, in 2006, my mother's sudden death hit me like a freight train.

The grief was too much to bear on top of everything else, and I dropped out of college. That decision came with a cost: I lost the progress I'd made and was left owing the school money. On top of that, I had racked up tens of thousands of dollars in student loans. The debt blocked me from returning to school, stalling my career, and leaving me stuck in jobs that didn't reflect my potential.

Wall Three: Despite the challenges, I always managed to keep steady employment and earned a decent salary, from the age of twenty-three.

But my financial habits were a mess. I made poor decisions, taking on credit I couldn't afford and frequently relying on payday loans just to buy groceries or pay for emergencies. These decisions wrecked my credit. Higher interest rates on everything kept me in a cycle of debt that was nearly impossible to escape. This financial instability built a wall that blocked me from achieving one of my biggest dreams— owning my own home.

There were days when I felt like life was a chessboard, and I'd made so many wrong moves that I'd checkmated myself with ill-thought-out decisions. I couldn't blame anyone but me. What's the saying? "If we knew better, we'd do better." But sometimes, even when we know better, desperation drives us to do the opposite, clinging to the hope that things will somehow work out in the end.

Deep down, I always believed I could overcome the toughest challenges. But there were moments when the consequences of my past decisions felt like walls closing in, suffocating any progress I tried to make. It was especially hard when I felt like I was standing on the edge of something big—on the verge of achieving my dreams—only to have those remnants of bad choices pull me back.

The saving grace was that I never let those walls define me. I held onto the hammer of personal growth with both hands, determined to chip away at those barriers, brick by brick. And no matter how long it took, I was committed to breaking free, demolishing every wall until I could finally walk into the life I knew I was destined to have.

Twenty

There's a scene in The Wiz that always stuck with me —when Dorothy learns that the power to return home was with her all along, right there in her ruby slippers. She didn't need the wizard or anyone else to save her; she just needed to believe in herself. I know I've reiterated this several times throughout this book, but it bears repeating for those in the back.

For much of my life, I was waiting for someone to hand me that same revelation, to give me permission to heal, grow, and step into my own light. But the truth is, the power to transform my life had been with me the whole time. My "ruby slippers" weren't just a metaphor—they were the inner strength and self-worth I'd carried all along.

When I turned my focus inward and committed to healing my emotional and psychological wounds, my life transformed in ways that felt nothing short of miraculous. I stopped blaming others for my circumstances and stopped waiting for someone to come and save me. Instead, I built myself up piece by piece, learning to see my worth and value from within.

And then, when I least expected it, love found me. Funny how life works that way. In 2007, I met the man who would become my twin soul, my partner, my equal. The beauty of it was that I wasn't looking for love; it came when I was focused on loving myself. This relationship wasn't about being rescued or completed—it was about being seen and supported.

Guess what happened to those walls? I started knocking them down, one by one.

In the summer of 1991, I was 21 years old and raising my three children when I decided at the last minute to get a summer job to bring in some extra cash. As part of the application process, I had to take a placement test. To the intake specialist's surprise, I scored in the highest percentile.

He looked at me in disbelief. "Have you tried to get your diploma?" he asked. When I shook my head, he leaned forward with a mix of encouragement and urgency. "With these scores, you don't even need classes. You should take the GED test immediately."

His words lit a spark in me. Without hesitation, I signed up for the last testing date of the season, barely making the deadline. On the day of the test, I walked into the center determined but nervous, wondering if I was truly prepared. I had been out of school almost four years and had heard horror stories of people failing on their first attempt.

Despite my doubts and insecurity, I passed the GED on my first try. That achievement felt like more than just a test score —it was the first brick removed from the wall of limitations I had unknowingly built around myself. It was proof that I was capable of more than I gave myself credit for.

Wall Two: In 2016, after over twenty years of starting, stopping, and starting again, I finally earned my bachelor's degree in education. It was a goal I had chased for so long, but life's hurdles always seemed to get in the way. Two years prior, my husband had encouraged me to reach out to the school to see if enrolling was even an option.

I was hesitant, weighed down by memories of being told years before that I couldn't register until my outstanding debt with the institution was paid in full.

But this time, I pushed past my fear of rejection and sent an email to admissions. To my surprise, they responded almost immediately, saying the process had changed—I was free to enroll. I was so overwhelmed with gratitude that I went straight to the school after work that day and signed up. And this time, I finished.

Earning my degree wasn't just about crossing a finish line—it was about breaking through barriers I'd built for far too long. For years, not having that diploma had felt like staring up at an unbreakable glass ceiling.

My potential was always limited by what I couldn't demand financially, what I couldn't claim professionally. But that "piece of paper," as one of my former managers once called it, shattered that ceiling and transformed the trajectory of my life. It wasn't just a milestone—it was a testament to persistence, faith, and second chances.

Within a few years of earning my degree, I broke through one of the biggest barriers in my professional life: landing my first six-figure job. I stepped into corporate America, working for one of the largest retail and logistics companies in the world. Before this, I had been trapped by the limitations of only having a high school equivalent diploma.

Time and again, employers had told me I couldn't be considered for management roles without a degree. For years, my professional growth felt like it was stuck in quicksand—until I made the decision to get out of my own way and invest in myself.

The financial boost from this career change sparked a domino effect that touched every corner of my life. With smarter planning and better opportunities, my credit score began to recover, my savings grew, and I finally allowed myself to dream beyond survival. I wasn't just keeping my head above water anymore; I was building a life with purpose and stability.

By 2023, I achieved something that once felt impossible: I built my own home, from the ground up. For a girl who grew up in an apartment with a shared bathroom, this wasn't just a milestone—it was a full-circle moment. Every detail, every bathroom I designed to my liking, reflected the journey that brought me there. My home became a tangible symbol of resilience, proof that I could rewrite my story and achieve the unimaginable.

But life isn't just triumphs; it's also trials. In 2018, the calm I'd worked so hard to create was shattered by a single phone call. My niece informed me that my brother, Durelle, was missing. In the months that followed, we searched tirelessly for him, holding on to the hope that he'd come back to us.

The truth, when it came, was devastating: my brother had been murdered. The loss was incomprehensible. I had already mourned the death of my mother in 2006, an experience that left an ache I thought could never be matched. Twelve years later, I found myself grieving all over again for my only brother.

The pain was suffocating, like a weight pressing down on my chest. Grief has a way of unraveling progress, testing the foundations of your strength in ways you're never prepared for. Losing my brother was one of those moments—a devastating blow that threatened to pull me under.

But instead of letting it consume me, I found resolve. I became more determined than ever to honor his memory and the expectations both he and my mother had for me. Their belief in me became my compass, guiding me through even the darkest days.

I think back to the pride in Mama's eyes when her ten-year-old daughter asked for a stamp and an envelope. I had written a thirty-page "novel" by hand and was determined to send it to Harlequin, the publishing company Mama adored for its romance and mystery books. With no computer or email back then, I waited weeks to hear back.

The rejection letter came, as expected, but it wasn't cold or dismissive—it encouraged me to stay in school and to keep writing. I like to imagine the person who sent it smiled at my passion and boldness, and saw a spark of the writer I would one day become.

Mama would be so proud to see that I never stopped writing. She'd beam knowing I now own a small publishing imprint, turning dreams I once thought were unreachable into reality.

Healing from life's trauma isn't a straight path. It's messy, nonlinear, and full of detours. But through every twist and turn, I've found reasons to keep going—gratitude for the love I've shared, wisdom from the lessons I've learned, and pride in the strength I've cultivated. Every step, even the painful ones, has brought me closer to who I am today.

This chapter of my life is one of continuous transformation. It's about letting go of self-doubt, embracing accountability, and creating a life rooted in both purpose and joy. It's about showing up for myself every day and building a legacy of hope and resilience for my children and grandchildren.

In The Wiz, there's a moment when Dorothy realizes the journey itself gave her the strength she needed to find her way. It wasn't the destination or a magic token—it was the courage, growth, and clarity she gained along the way. That's what I've come to understand about my own life: every challenge, every heartbreak, every hard-fought lesson was shaping me, preparing me for the success I was meant to achieve.

As I step into the next chapter, I do so with gratitude for my past experiences, faith in my own resilience, and excitement for what's to come. Because if life has taught me anything, it's this: the road may be winding, but it's the journey that defines us, and the best is still ahead.

Epilogue

The past shapes us, but we can't let it define us. Reflecting on my journey—the good, the bad, and everything in between—has taught me this truth: every experience holds a lesson, and those lessons mold us into who we are and who we're still becoming.

For me, looking back isn't about dwelling on the pain or mistakes; it's about acknowledging the path I've walked and the strength I've gained along the way.

I know I'm blessed. God has saved me more times than I can count, often in ways I didn't fully understand at the time. But there have been moments when His presence was unmistakable. I think about the house fire that could have claimed my life. I remember two severe car accidents I walked away from with barely a scratch.

And there are countless other instances where one wrong move could have been deadly. Yet here I am, alive and standing. These weren't coincidences—they were reminders that I am here for a purpose, and I am determined to fulfill it.

The pains of my past, whether caused by my own choices or circumstances beyond my control, are no longer weights dragging me down—they are lessons lifting me up. The greatest lesson of all is this: never let yourself become a victim of circumstances.

Victims stay stuck in their pain, drowning in discontent. Survivors rise, dust themselves off, and keep moving forward. I am a survivor, and as long as I have breath in my body, I'll keep fighting—not just for myself, but for my mother and my brother.

My mother was a fighter. I saw the weariness in her eyes, heard it in her voice, and watched physical fatigue slowly take her down. But she never gave up. That spirit of resilience, that unyielding determination, is her greatest gift to me. It's what gave me the strength to face the storms life placed in my path.

To the young people reading this: your individuality and independence are treasures. You won't make all the right choices—no one does. But give yourself the grace to make mistakes, learn from them, and then move forward. Life is a journey, not a destination.

To adults who feel stuck: ask yourself why. But don't stop at the question—take action. Get in the driver's seat of your life. Take the wheel, press the gas, and start driving. You don't need to know your destination right away; sometimes, it's the journey that matters. The power to move forward lies within you.

To parents: our children grow up to be who they want to be, not who we want them to be. Our job is to teach, guide, and lay the foundation. Beyond that, arm them with knowledge, especially about breaking cycles that may run in your family. After that, it's up to them. Some kids bloom early, some bloom late, and sadly, some don't bloom at all. We do our best, but adulthood is their journey to navigate.

Purpose drives us. It keeps us going when life feels unbearable, when the ache in our hearts tempts us to give in to despair. Whether through faith, hope, or sheer determination, purpose gives us the strength to keep moving forward.

We are here for a reason. When you discover that reason, you find your wings. And when you find your wings, you take flight. Ruby slippers are for those who need shoes to keep their feet on the ground. But when you fly, you don't need shoes. You just soar.

References

The following sources have informed the statistics and insights included throughout this memoir:

National Domestic Violence Hotline

Information on abuse and the dynamics of abusive relationships.

Website: www.thehotline.org

Rape, Abuse & Incest National Network (RAINN)

Statistics on sexual assault and the importance of seeking counseling.

Website: www.rainn.org

National Institute on Drug Abuse (NIDA)

Research on the effects of substance abuse and addiction on individuals and families.

Website: www.drugabuse.gov

Centers for Disease Control and Prevention (CDC)

Insights on trauma, mental health, and the prevalence of childhood abuse.

Website: www.cdc.gov

U.S. Department of Education

Data on GED attainment and its impact on career opportunities.

Website: www.ed.gov

National Center for Education Statistics (NCES)

Research on high school dropout rates and the long-term effects on earning potential.

Website: www.nces.ed.gov

Substance Abuse and Mental Health Services Administration (SAMHSA)

Resources for individuals and families dealing with mental health and substance abuse.

Website: www.samhsa.gov

American Psychological Association (APA)

Studies on the psychological effects of childhood trauma and abuse.

Website: www.apa.org

The National Coalition Against Domestic Violence (NCADV)

Statistics and resources on domestic violence in the United States.

Website: www.ncadv.org

The World Health Organization (WHO)

Global data on the effects of abuse and addiction on health and well-being.

Website: www.who.int

These references provide additional context for the themes explored in Ruby Slippers: Fairy Tales My Mother Told Me, Secrets I Never Shared. For further reading or support, please visit the websites listed above.

About the Author

Michelle Davis-Newell is a passionate storyteller whose journey reflects resilience, determination, and an unwavering belief in second chances. Born and raised on Chicago's South Side, Michelle discovered a love for writing in her youth, which became a lifelong passion.

In 2007, she self-published her debut novel, Ain't Understanding Mellow?, followed by the first edition of her deeply personal memoir, Ruby Slippers: Fairy Tales My Mother Told Me, Real Life Truths I Never Told Her, in 2013. In 2024, Michelle published The Bag Ladies of Ebondale under ScribeRite Publishing LLC, the publishing company she co-founded with her husband.

This updated edition of Ruby Slippers revisits and expands on her original memoir, breathing new life into her story while continuing to inspire readers.

Michelle's career path has been as dynamic as her writing. She spent 24 years in social services, where she developed programs to empower at-risk youth, including mock trials and creative workshops. Separately, she co-wrote and co-produced the short film Roses Out of Concrete, shot in her beloved Bronzeville community.

Today, she works as a senior manager for one of the largest global online retailers, bringing the same determination and creativity to her leadership role.

In 2016, at the age of 46, Michelle fulfilled a promise to her late mother by earning her bachelor's degree in education, proving it's never too late to achieve your goals. This accomplishment not only shifted her career trajectory but also deepened her commitment to inspiring others.

When she's not working or writing, Michelle treasures time with her family, especially her grandchildren, and shares her home with her husband, their bonus son, and their Pomeranian, Bruno Mars.

Fairy Tale & The Wiz Reference Guide

Throughout Ruby Slippers: Fairy Tales My Mother Told Me, Secrets I Never Shared, both direct and indirect references to timeless fairy tales and the iconic story of The Wiz are woven into the narrative to illustrate themes of resilience, self-discovery, and personal transformation. This guide offers brief summaries for readers who may not be familiar with these stories.

Fairy Tale References

Cinderella

Summary: Cinderella is a young woman who overcomes a life of servitude under her cruel stepmother and stepsisters. With the help of her fairy godmother, she attends a royal ball, capturing the prince's heart. Despite challenges, her kindness and perseverance lead to her happily-ever-after.

Themes: Transformation, resilience, and finding hope in the face of adversity.

Goldilocks and the Three Bears

Summary: Goldilocks is a curious girl who ventures into the forest and enters the house of three bears while they're away. She tests their porridge, chairs, and beds, seeking what feels "just right." The bears return, and she learns a lesson about boundaries and consequences.

Themes: Curiosity, exploration, and learning through experience.

Sleeping Beauty

Summary: A princess cursed to fall into a deep sleep is saved by a prince's kiss. Sleeping Beauty's tale emphasizes the importance of patience and the triumph of good over evil.

Themes: Renewal, awakening, and perseverance through trials.

The Ugly Duckling

Summary: A young bird, mocked for his appearance, endures hardship before transforming into a beautiful swan. His journey highlights the value of inner strength and self-acceptance.

Themes: Self-worth, transformation, and recognizing inner beauty.

The Wiz References

The Wiz is a beloved retelling of The Wizard of Oz, featuring an all-Black cast and a soulful, vibrant reimagining of the classic story. Its themes of courage, self-discovery, and unity resonate deeply. Key characters referenced include:

Dorothy

Role: A young woman swept away by a tornado to the magical land of Oz. She journeys to find her way home, discovering her inner strength along the way.

Quote Inspiration: Dorothy's journey reminds us that the solutions we seek often lie within us.

The Scarecrow

Role: Believing himself to be unintelligent, the Scarecrow learns he has always possessed the wisdom and resourcefulness he seeks.

Quote Inspiration: "You've had the brains all along" emphasizes trusting one's abilities.

The Tin Man

Role: Convinced he has no heart, the Tin Man demonstrates compassion throughout the journey, showing that love resides within him.

Quote Inspiration: "You've had a heart all along" reminds us of our inherent capacity for love.

The Cowardly Lion

Role: Despite his fears, the Lion discovers his courage while protecting his friends.

Quote Inspiration: "You've had the courage all along" highlights bravery in the face of fear.

The Ruby Slippers

Role: These magical shoes symbolize the power Dorothy holds to control her destiny.

Quote Inspiration: "You've always had the power to go home" is a metaphor for self-reliance and inner strength.

These stories serve as metaphors, reflecting the challenges and triumphs of real life. They remind us that, like the characters in these tales, we all have the power to rise above obstacles, discover our strengths, and write our own happily-ever-after.